Weaves & Yarns

Donal O'Connell

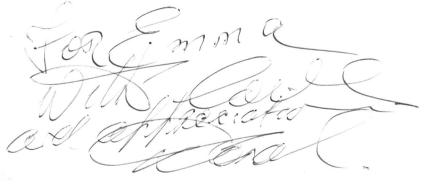

For my children

Anna, Denise, Lisa, Danielle, Naomi, Curnán.

Contents

The Spirit of the Universe

What worlds mysterious roll within the vast,
The all-encircling ocean of the mind!
Cup-like thereon our form are floating fast,
Only to fill and sink and leave behind
No spray of bubbles from the Sea up-cast.

The spirit thou canst not view, it comes so nigh,
Drink of this Presence! Be not thou a jar
Laden with water, and its lip stone- dry;
Or as a horseman blindly borne afar,
Who never sees the horse beneath his thigh.

Rumi.

"What can be attained is the elimination of privilege. This is really the work before the whole world. In all social lives, there has been one fight in every race and in every country. The difficulty is not that one body of men are naturally more intelligent than another, but whether this body of men, because they have advantage of intelligence, should take away even physical enjoyment from those who do not possess that advantage. The fight is to destroy that privilege."
Vivekananda

The lock of error shuts the gate,
Open it with the key of love;
Thus, by opening the door,
Thou shall wake the Beloved.
Kabir says:"O brother!do not pass
By such good fortune as this."

Kabir.

Tipp for Races

When Galway's western tribes go into eastern mode,
Embracing the Indochinese compulsion intensity for incestuous gambling,
An almost death wish bordering on Russian roulette,
Hangs like Havana cigar smoke, in the licensed premises,
Bedazzling the women, mesmerizing the men,
Weaving spells of no tomorrow with black outs of yesterday.
Then old ghosts hold sway and have their way traipsing, tricking,
Trolloping down the blocked up back alleys
Near Quay Street and Buttermilk Lane.
                              Yes it's Race Week!
While question mark terror hangs there remotely beckoning,
Mockingly daring, insanely encouraging the smouldering virgin eyes of young ones,
Who too have tasted spirits incautiously and seek further exploration.   Luring longings,
dancing dares in prolonged titillation,
Awaiting first hand excitation,
Not all the jockeys are on the race course!
Is your daughter dressed up as a Shop Street Slapper ?
While you lurk in the shadows of Bishop Brown's last Erection?

In denial of how you got the clean spotless-
white clean stiff shirt
 From the incarcerated Magdalene girls and their
bonneted jailers?
Aieeh! Hurts it does to recognize that denial is
not just a river in Egypt that's far away.
Or can it be swept under the carpet like Bertie's
Bankers hellicoptering the West coast, hoovering
for speculation sites with our dough,
Oh no mmmmm !
Yes, it will happen again, 'cause you will
continue
To court for further favours condemning us to
debt.

Race week 2012

The Toiler

Wakes he does
From unease
Eats he does
From habit
Masticates he does
To balance
Balances he does
To ask for more.
Thinks he does
To disguise motives
Thinks again he does
To conceal the real
Shuffles he does
Between the thoughts.
Pities he does
To smother the infant
Languish he does
Having drowned the child
Drinks he does
To wash the shame

Drinks again he does
To fix the blame.
Blame he does
To alter the balance

Numbs he does
To freeze the confusion
Procrastinates he does
To avoid reality
Toils he does
To maintain the avoidance.

Thinking like a Native Nicene Frenchman

With my back to the snug in "Rue Droite"
On the corner by Rue Rossetti
Facing down to Egles St. Jaques
I await surrender and observe the out of towners
Arrive with their black leather jackets slung
Lazily over their shoulders.
They have just parked their motor cycles and helmets
To allow more freedom on the pedestrian narrow
Streets of Old Nice.
The streets here are ablaze of colour
Clogged by the myriads of small galleries
Displaying in carnival fashion designs to dazzle,
Dimensions to startle, and moods to amuse and muse over.
The cobbled streets have history locked in the crevices
Between the stones while ever so often after a downpour
Eerie figments and strange vagaries emanate in shadow
Carrying me away from the Old Town.
So down the road by the sea I found myself
Sitting on my ass in the *"reilig"*of Holy Trinity Church in Rue de Bouef.
I close my eyes and listen to my hair curling in static crackling,

And feel the fractured nature in my vicinity.
Sensing some restlessness of fellow spirits
Like some echoing of banter and repartee with
accompaniment of
Some cooing pigeons, tweeting sparrows and
warblers,
I know its time to pause, reflect, research and
rediscover what drew me here.
An elaborate sarcophagus draped in a carved
stone cloak and opened books,
Four pedestals like horse hoofs, to gallop
through eternities by-ways.
Here among the tombstones are the melting
bones of other Gaelic ramblers.
One a traveller from the 1800's, buried here with
his wife Naomi
Beside another stray from Ballyfinn.
What hooked them here to this healing town of
Nice?
Is it the mannerly camaraderie I encounter as I
meander the multitude of friendly streets,
Markets, cafés, bars and restaurants?
A Marquise, Caroline de Messing, daughter of
Sir Charles Coote, of Ballyfinn House, young she
was just 29   years, having
completed her full course with Saturn
Up to the ninth of June 1848.
Followed in shortly by Richard Warburton, from
Garryhinch in 1852.
Now here we are parallel to" Promenade des
Anglaise et Irlandaise? "ausie je quais!."
Those Warburton's from Garryhinch scattered
their seed while travelling widely
Performing noble deeds, while flying high in
unison with "The Wild Geese".

The calling of Durini from India got answered
like "dent du lion"on the wind
Over the Himalayas –Will it be A? Will it be B?
Will it be C? Oh!! It's D!
Oft to be found – for some, romance is "would
you like to be buried with my people"?

Villefranche sur Mer

Changed it is completely,
(Apart from the Rue Obscure, and the hero
galley slave's wood carving of the crucified
Jesus).
Populated today with rich tourists
And people catering for rich tourists.
The life blood of camaraderie flowed out to sea
With the departure of the old navy.
The girls who were so friendly
And undercharged each other,
Are gone to foreign climes
But now replaced by dames respectable
In hard commerce, extractors of the dime.
Yes, times have changed
And values differ
Viagra has come and men are stiffer,
While the upper lip quivers
For righteous wages,
You got nothing for nothing
Throughout the ages.
These career dames in designer jackets
Who looked down on those who played with
sailors
Are not so different in what they do for wages.
Secure and snug with society's backing,
Laughter, fun, song and joy are lacking.
Those long stepped stairs
That climbed the hill,
They held the heat at night from scorching sun,

And released it later, to those bodies who
faltered
And failed to catch the late night bus,
Having had their fill.
A wide step was an adequate pillow
To sleep till dawn,
The morning sun would ring alarm
To hurry up and catch the early bus to work
again
For wages, and play the games
With buxom dames
Having lots of fun and frolics,
And "eh dasseur" to those that judge
You're nothing but a bollix.

Who is this Guy?

Who is this guy inside my body
Who is now enjoying the dawn chorus?
Having spent his youth reviling the avian
revellers
While nodding off in drunken stupor to the
sounds of
Clip clopping hoof beats and clinking bottles
from
The milkman's trolley cart.
Who is this guy? Who as a boy
Rebelled and resented
Command callers and finger pointers of
judgement,
While now he smiles and nods in daily
greetings,
To the wearers of navy blue and black uniforms
With their dog collars and silver buttons, despite
The painful recall of past injustices,
He bids them all a lovely day!
Who is this guy who throbs now with joy
And inside my body lurks
And smirks at my disdain
For the tabernacle keepers who
Seemingly know naught of the "Name in Vain"
To which they refer in their second of ten,
Again and again.
How do I know? I do not know!
But sure I am of my origin
At the source of all creation,
That little speck that beckons me home in a

Welcome conflagration, exploding and
imploding
In exuberance within,.
Yes, within the confines of this corporeal form,
Exists a microcosm, of the macrocosm without.
How do I know? I do not know! But know I do
for sure,
That God is love and love is God and that Truth
will so endure.
My mind is the battleground where my and
mine and false notions
Of permanence entertain the *maya.

*illusion
27/05/2007

Dogs on the Road

Once upon a time when the world seemed to revolve more slowly, people had light heartedness in all their greetings, dogs tails constantly wagged, then we had a world that really was worth living in. Dandelions and daisies were in abundance and little girls were always making long, long daisy chains Small boys had short trousers with crusty scabby knees that were always just about to bleed, there were yellow green streaks from wrist to elbow on their pullovers and had those opaque bubbles in suspension from the nostrils which were punctuated with a regular sniff at the beginning and end of each sentence. Attentive dogs lolled nearby, they, never having seen, or known a collar, or even imagined such a thing as "neuter". A ride in the middle of the road always got the crowd going, and after a few good guffaws, all the auld lads headed for the pub.

The rest stayed out for pitch and toss with heavy pennies, if you got it right and barred them, you were made.   A good race down the street with four or five lads beating *bowlies was hard to beat for excitement then. Come to think of it, there was a lot of widow women back then, grey hair or raven black to match the black black shawl and there was always a brazen one with a tilted head and a flaming headscarf. They cackled among themselves and always killed the fun with buckets of cold water over the grinning dogs.

  *old bicycle wheel rims

Lou Lou

A Liverpudlian young lassie with gorgeous red
hair,
A wistful eye she had, and she looked from over
there.
She is busy clearing tables,
Serving tourists on holiday,
She is young, fresh and innocent,
With freckles on her face,
Glad to earn the few bob,
At Paddy's Point – that's the place.
Outside you have chairs, parasols and tables,
Providing welcome shade on a scorching
afternoon,
The punters watch horse racing with call over,
Swilling beer to quench their thirst,
While young Sheona our new young waitress,
Tilts her head and arches eyebrow,
As they swear and do their worst.
I came back some two weeks later,
She smiled with a welcome grin,
Thanked me for that first day's encouragement,
Said she had learned a lot since then.
I loved her look of innocence
And the curl on her freckled brow,
A tiny stud now sparkled by her nostril,

She wagged her head to say "you see"
I nodded my approval, it looked good!
But "tattoos were not to be"!
For me, a sweet memory of young innocence,
In a darling little Liverpudlian baby.

No Pain No Gain

The tour bus arrives in Tranquilville,
Disgorges old agers, middle agers, and recent
divorcees.
They plod possessively towards their gendered
assesos,
Grudgingly, furtively, guarding their place.
Lavabo, behind them, they join in the queue,
Silently seething they have nothing to do
But stuff themselves silly and wait by the door,
Of another *assesos* with pee on the floor.
Age has crept up,
Divorce has not freed,
What's been trying to escape
Has held on with greed
In the need for possessions
To heal all with gain
'Puts a weight in the bowel
That's pleading for strain
Release from the tension by getting away
No one gets off that easy
You too have to pay.

(Among the also ran Spain '09)

Morning Balcony Observances

Caw- caw -caw , tweet-tweet-twee,
Caw- caw- caw-caw,twee – twe- tweeee,
Caw- caw, twee -e-e-e-ee-eeee tweet, tweeet.
Palm trees sway in deep pendulum rhythm
Pronouncing their top heaviness.
The waves beat the shore and dissipate their pound
Into an audible shuddering.
Jay Lee (caretaker) sweeps, sweeps and sweeps
And sweeps and sweeps and sweeps,
The withered crinkly crackly leaves
And the all prevailing freshly landed red dust.
The long boned Indian yoga teacher
In his knee-length white dhoti
Has the rapt attention of the
Western white maidens
As they stretch on the nearby flat rooftop
Amidst the palms and electric wires
While their rickshaw drivers await at the gate
And grab an hour's doze on their own back seats.
Meanwhile salutations to the sun
Stretch towards new awareness.

22/1/05. (Samudra Tara, Lighthouse Beach)

Just Before Leaving Kolkata

I continue to dangle like a spider in suspension.
Any breeze that blows will alter my direction.
Feelings are within- just beneath the surface.
*"Quo Vadis," the prompter niggles?
There is a pause in my surrender
And I am prompted to reel up home
Where it may be safe.
Fear and insecurity have been my fellow
travelers,
But have not been given rein to ruin.
This love that frees me
From the world that is insane.
OK, so I don't know where I am going,
But my destination is home.
The light and love is clear there
With the sound and the taste at one with Aum,
A new breath for surrender in whatever breeze
that blows.

*whither goest thou?

January 3rd 2004

Parúnth Overlooking Lighthouse Beach

The caw caw stops short
When he is really near.
His arrival is swift decisive
Alights, grabs, wrestles
Black feathers fly
As certain palm tree perches
He declares unequivocally to be sacrosanct.
This sea eagle *parúnth*,
This high flying surveyor
Shares not his landing strip
With caw caw scavengers.
His circling presence is felt below.
His shadow silences the twee twees .
His large wedge tail declares power steering.
His wide wingspan makes for effortless soaring
On elevator currents to an eerie penthouse
Frequented only by his own kin.
This hawk headed shriller
Looks you in the eye without flinch.

parúnth colloquial term for sea eagle in
Malayalam
 pronounced parúnthá.

28/01/05

The Lamplighter

A parched and perished scorched to the skut
wick,

Protrudes like a piece of bog oak on a desert
landscape.

Lonely yet resigned to the kindness of the
constant erosion

Brought about by time in solitude,

Patiently awaiting the perfect permanent
lamplighter.

Sandgrained, stubbed and stubborn while
silently sighing

For the soothing sound of the fluttering flame

To fan and flare the fragrant heart.

How does he come and when does he come?

 This lamplighter

From Gu to Ru is night and day

Is black to white and darkness light.

The journey –

Uncovering, discovering, discarding

What is not maya in this world?

Is so, so simple and so, so slight

That one might easily pass it by.

6/12/03.

Warm Bones

The Sun streams down
And soaks right in through my skin
Warming the bones.
These bones have lived in the cold
In the dark deprived areas
Where living entities perished in utter isolation
Crushed and mutilated calcified rock to stardust
And edging forward again through embryo
Into life encountering the ever-changing
Ongoingness of creation.
Perceptible *prana* pulsating in primordial
Perpetuational courses and intercourses
From tailbone to frontal lobe
Lapping with lingering longings for sanctuary.
A place of rest and tranquil fulfillment
Constantly churning excitement in the chakras.

Spain 10/3/09.   *prana life force*

Opera Plage in Mid-October

The sun shines and sparkles on a wide angel's
highway,
Where airplanes ascend from Nice airport.
Some sailboats pass quite close to shore
While most are nearer the horizon.
This stony beach is still strewn with female sun
worshippers
Earphone listening on their Ipods
With British gay boys airing their views
Loudly and brashly enough to proclaim their
Bulldog origins and imperial heritage
They swagger openly in their gender certainty
Apart from home, away from ridicule.
Swiss, British, French, Italian flags fly over
Opera Plage.
Young lady French girl protrudes her navel
Pierced with a gold ring to her well tanned,
White bikinied, admiring companion,
They chat a while, while the pierced one walks
on,
The well tanned stretches for more sunshine.
Black miniature poodle with pompom tail
Bounces cheerfully, chasing stones thrown by
bespectacled proud lady owner,
While pigeons skitter among the stones seeking
Crumbs from old and semi-devoured, half-
buried snacks.
Now granddad has gone out to sea – at last

Where buoyancy has relieved the pain
Of traversing stones from too much weight
And neglected good intentions.
Now some fishing rods have made the scene
Supported by their tripods,
While the casters cast with little hope
Of expectation to procure their supper,
But they kill the time and parade in line
Conversing with each other.
Beach chatter is broken by the grumbling
Sound of a heavy jet just left the ground
And heading skywards – and just now has
Disappeared from view and wandered
Off into the blue direct for destination.
Mr Japan strides forward with his
One- foot long camera projecting his technology
For further exploration.
My partner is ambling along the shore,
She is searching for me, of that I am sure
For I have the money, passports and key of the
door.

15th October, 2010   15.42

Holy Communion

I miss that country of millions of villages
Where the earth smell is unmistakable
Where the wag of the head is affirmative
And time stands with you in queue.
The noise and clamour of daily life
And the myriad colours in the hustle and bustle
Of hubbub traffic in it's cooperating chaos,
The searching eyes of the streetwise survivors
On the constant alert for opportunity awaiting
cue.
The ever-prompting whispers from the alleys
Alluding to what could occur and had happened
In less fortunate times – Yes.
And yes I miss those pleading plucking
Hands that remind me that remind me,
That remind me deeply, of how fortunate
I am this lifetime out.
Ah! But I miss being there among them,
A part of them, connected in communion.

Dawn 4/10/08. Turlough

Down At Heel

These worn old sandals that
Walked for months of miles
On the red dust of India,
All along the marshy backwater
Kingfisher pathways of Kerala
Through the waves, surf and the
Never-ending beaches of Goa,
Leading arse biting, two hump camels
Into Pushkar, Rajasthan.
On the banks of holy Ganges in Banares
Plodding mazes of back streets down
Cow dung alleys echoing some haunting bhjans
That lured me like the pied piper
Or a hurried worried hamster on a wheel
In perpetuum mobile.
Shuffling with shadow men among the stalls
Along the Khaosarn Road for Bangkok bargains,
Chasing six foot flimsy figments among
The brightest warmest smiles in colorful Fiji-
Busy buzzing while slinging hammocks
On island ferries while biking in Cambodia.
Hurting hips in the Atlas Mountains after
Riding one hump camels in Tunisia,
Laughing in luxury while limping
Around Lisboa
Spread-eagling over Espagne and Canaria
Steadfastly promising to lighten the load
On these old sandals, these old sandals

That are now heel thin and hurting
As I encounter the stony beach underfoot
Opposite Promenade des Anglaise
Back in Nice.
Manana, manana, manana
Again the promise to slim
Down to where I was when
Last I prowled this promenade
In wild lustful days
Over two score years ago.

"and she thinks they are scruffy
old hippy sandals-bin overdue"

Nice July 09

Crinkly Eyes

Yes you dared to smile at me with those crinkly
eyes
Bold and daring, no thought of homey husband.
Ah! Yes your submerged passion surfaced
silently
And slid forth from beneath those folds of
finery,
While that look of wild abandon, of untamed
freedom,
Reached forward for potential realization.
Redolently you retracted, reluctantly relaxed,
You regarded the current vista,
As maybe currently unwise,
Under the circumstances.
Now let me say – your brief foray in
Circuitous navigation,
May in the future lead to unrestrain,
And put in train a passion for appeasement.
Oh! English rose, "ma fleur de lis" your pulse,
Your pulse, that tiny fleck beside those crinkly
eyes,
That imploring impulse –daring,
May be the cause of some new wooing,
For I know, that pulse beside your eye
Betrays another inside your thigh
That lures a lad to fondle,
And kindles the spark to maybe ramble.

Midnight Dipping

I saw a young girl at a work bench on TV
She was the very image of my long-ago love
Noree.
Ah! The movement of her hands!
The inclination of her head, Oh!
Those furrows on her brow,
She choked me up.
So swallowing hard,
I retreat in my solitude
And resurrect that adventurous excitement
That nudged the scales and tipped the balance
To venture out beyond the confines of strict
matrimony
To explore the shore
And swim out much more without impediment..
Erect and pert with narrow girth she shimmered.
In the moonlight she flowed and glistened
And we listened to lonely waves lap on a strand,
Unfettered by society band that ominous
restriction.

A New Relationship - maybe

I am cold, angry, frustrated confused.
It's Saturday night
I feel isolated alone
It's my own fault.
Here I am unable to state
That I have needs in a relationship
To know roughly what is happening
And where do I fit in on her list.
I feel shrunk, analyzed and misunderstood.
I have declared myself honestly
Maybe honestly to a fault -
The vulnerability that ensues
Is made more acute by some subconscious
Expectation of reciprocation
Of equal openness.
"Well my serenity is inversely proportionate
To my expectations " - I know!!
No mans land is a lonely place,
I could wallow in self pity
Pillaging among throw away platitudes.
I am tired of not having a home,
A fire to warm my bones
A pair of hands to knead my aching back.
The thought to join the shop doorway shufflers,
With their newspaper lined trousers,

Cardboard mattresses and brown paper bag hot-
water bottle
To swish down the venom
And regurgitate the unpronounceable injustices
The thought leers masochistically from a familiar
sense
Of foreboding and impending doom,
The fuck it switch comes on the brain
And the thought to sabotage
All that one holds dear seems acceptable.
Again I know that the exes indicative phone call
Has greased a downward spiral of
malcontentment
To the gulley and the gutter.

16th March, 2002.

Magpie

That black and white
Helicopter bird
That flies straight across my window
A cheeky strut he has
Like a headwaiter
From a bygone age.

The lawn is his in the early morn
Where he pronounces his dominance
Uttering sharp chock choke cries
Displaying pointed tattoo stampings of
impatience
He shoos away all intruders
Even the cat gives a wide berth
Cotton trails of mist and eerie fog puffs still
linger
In the chill early dawn
Promising an eventful day
One for sorrow, two for Joy!

My Dorrie

Yes she was mine,
The feeling came back like as if it was yesterday.
I closed my eyes
And time diminished
But she remained intact and warm.
I was her wee man
In under her dressing gown
Outside on the flat roof
Held tight, snug cuddled.
A frosty moonlit night with sparkly stars
Was up there, out there, where her soldier boy
was
She brought me out, so I could be with him too.
She hummed and sang the wireless war songs
And I felt lonely with her and a little sad
Why? Because she was sad,
Her laugh was missing and that was rare.
Dorrie took me for walks every day
When I woke at night, she was there
To tell me stories, to cuddle beside me
Because I had only me and Don the dog,
The baby that was to be my brother or sister
Wasn't coming any more,
And Daddy was always different in his uniform,
Mummy's eyes were far away and dreamy sad
angry.
I still miss you Dorrie.!

Nothing Worthwhile out there

* "Taimse ag teacht abhaile",
I learned to stand,
To clutch and move,
All the time looking,
Seeking searching for more,
More what?
Satisfaction, fulfillment,
Happiness, contentment
Moving out
Motivation always more
A kind of greed
Of course I called it need
And on it went -
Through school, through college
Through games, drink, drugs, career
Through sex, through religion,
Through marriage,
All the time outside myself,
Through knowledge
Knowledge of what?
"I once knew ",
Knew when I was happy and content
And trusted life
For my breath to come and go
And come again
Renewing life

Making a fresh start
On each breath
A wondrous potential
Unfolding surrender
My awareness to *grá*
To *grá,* attitude to gratitude,
Returning home,
Having looked clearly at what's outside,
Assessed and accepted without fear of loss.

*I'm coming home.

October '07.

Oge

When I am feeling lonely
I am most real
Feeling that isolation and aloneness
And breathing it in deep
Allows me to revolve and circumnavigate
My memory banks from birth to now.
Trembling in my own uniqueness
Excited by the loss and self severance
From my attachments and reciprocal
reassurances
Of insecure fellow creatures
The glowing cool light of truth shines
Back from my reflection while I breathe
My breaths in solitary gratitude -
A traveler ready for solo space in sanctuary.
What did I find here worthwhile?
Some few who put the Grá in gratitude
The aghá in awesome and the wow in
wonderful.

August '09.

Karnatakan Soul Traveller

Yes Sangita you still swirl
And twirl that seductive body
Peering cautiously and alarmingly
Brazenly lazily languid
In furtive fantasy weaving
And gently jangling
Those tinkle bells that lure
The inquisitive pilgrim to
Venture and see beyond
Your colourful gypsy costume,
Your multi pierced organs pronounce
An adventurous spirit way beyond
My western culture boundaries.
Your eyes direct probing
Lacerate   some of my soul's
Bandages and expose some
Tender areas wherein, in my
Meanderings, I never ventured.
That infant son of yours who
Bounced on my knee whooping
Playfully at the sound of my harmonica
As you sewed up my trousers on
Your hand sewing machine
You made me feel part of your little family
Just for a moment, as you stroked my arm
While smiling without guile or agenda.
As I stroll now the strand, with my shoes in
hand

Through these cool Atlantic waters
I touch your ringed toes across the oceans
And remember how we swapped stories
Of our happy carefree childhoods,
I told you about Newgrange and you told me
About the Indus Valley Civilizations 3000 B.C.
Our toes played together in the sand
Peeking slightly beyond innocence,
My throat lumped and you spotted it
With those liquid violet eyes of yours,
And we agreed we really liked one another.

A White Witness in the Snow

Softly gently silently it falls
The flakes are ever so small
Compact and dense in their falling,
There is no abatement
Visibility is somewhat foggy.
The clock on the wall
Very audibly ticks out its seconds
It is now twenty to noon
On this epiphany festive day of
Birthdays for my daughter Siv
And her twelve year younger brother Curnán.
She takes her well earned rest
And awaits the arrival of her children
While he adventures
On the ski slopes with her boyfriend.
I am proud of these young people
And know that future generations
Will remember them for their intelligent
Forthright unquestionable integrity
Their kindness humour and sense of fun and
Mischief and their courageous open dealings.
Ancestral genes are gallantly enshrined and
insured
And I will gladly rest content
That no ambiguity will prevail or trail
To taint our ancestors,

(*Nollaig na mBan*, 6th. January, 2011, in Sweden)

Commotion Promotion

The nine year old will cry no more,
Defiantly he looks to fore,
Determined that no tear will drop
To please the Christian Brother sadist with the
strap.
Now Brother D's soutane is squeaky clean,
His black shoes are polished bright,
His dark curly hair is neatly combed,
He wears a gold 'Fainne'
And speaks 'as Gaeilge' in a precise clipped
tone,
Tight eyes burn with frustration from living
alone.
This young cur before him he will punish!
He will rue the day! He will make him pay!
From the pocket of the cassock the leather pokes,
The lad is before the class to be humiliated in
exhibition,
A pin can be heard to drop in the tin shed
classroom,
Save for the draught of flame hissing from the
pot-bellied stove.
Silence prevails; all the boys except the lad look
downwards,
His teeth are clenched to take six of the best.
The lad thinks to himself 'it's always like this on
a Monday,
Someone has to get it.
This time it's me, we'll see can I numb the pain?

Stop the shame! No one cares! No one dares!
We'll see!
The first five strokes were brought down hard.
Suspension for a moment, just to breathe,
To cry would have been a joy, release for a little boy.
'T was not to be, 'cause the sixth stroke numbed
Those senses that were to be suppressed
And the lad had not cried and he felt blessed!
So he put out for more, to use up the store
Of vehemence from within, while Brother D. snarled,
A cur!, A pup! You'll pay! Today!
Six more were delivered without delay,
He panted for breath, little spits or sweat!
He rolled up his sleeve to get a better swing,
While the lad looked out to his pals in their desks,
All but one feared to look up, in case they were next.
Cuddy Ken looked forward to support his friend,
There was never this many!, it had to end,
But stop it did not it went on and on,
Until all the little faces looked up to see,
White foamy flecks frothing from Brother D.,
While the lads eyes were smiling,
Pain was felt no more.
The little boy won!?? He held the floor.
He'd cry no more!.

Firebrigade

Goose, Tiny, Deadeye and Boyce
The boys from the "Firebrigade" I remember
them well.
I arrived at a monastery in early January
To be greeted by the gropey monk Hoppy
Who ushered me with my sheets and blankets
To the special dormitory for the disturbed boys
The troublesome ones
Who came from dysfunctional backgrounds.
Most of these lads were bedwetters,
teethgrinders,
Sleepwalkers and sleeptalkers.
The dean of discipline from my last school
Had classed me as a depraved delinquent.
Well that judgemental bully priest
Had cast me in a role –a pigeon hole,
An identity I was yet to reach for many years
later
When outlaw feelings from separation
Castigation and denunciation overwhelmed.
No – I was another soul in pain
Among the misunderstood
Who were put away, locked away
For our own good – so we were told.
Now Deadeye was a dribbler
With a very runny nose
He had overlapping teeth
And wore very country clothes
One eye wandered east while the other
Checked the west and then he crossed them,

When it was best to be silent.
He spoke like a machine gun,
So so so anxious to pe pe pe please and be
understood.
He was gentle and courageous
Bright intelligent with a brain
But his treatment was inane -
And to watch him smile as the "Wild Colonial
Boy"
Who came from Castlemaine was sung
Was a joy, was such a joy for me a very lonely
boy.
Now Goose was quite a gander
He was slightly red and touchy to say the least,
That was on the outside
But Mr. sensitive deep within,
He missed his mother dearly but
His father not so much
For he had that heavy touch.
Now Boycee was out there big time
Sought to please and be placated for
Wrongs that were never done-
Resentments stuck and wrinkled his brow
And made him prone to seek oblivion
In the animal kingdom all alone.
Then Tiny cool and dextrous kept
His mind unto himself, picked all brains
In his vicinity and aimed for the upper shelf
Waved a scalpel in the science lab and
announced
His destiny –a surgeon sure for certain.

Now some forty years later,

Deadeye slightly stuttered while on the back stairs
Of the firebrigade - Doc says he, do you remember?,
And I did, and he did too, while Boycee died
From his resentments - just avoiding a wet brain,
While Tiny and Goose shifted uneasily as we sang
"The Wild Colonial Boy" from Deadeye's town
A place called Castlemaine.

23/5/12.

The Slick Slider

Aboard the slick slider between Galway and
Dublin
We dribble out of the station
Across the permanently under repair bridge
That spans a lazy Lough Atalia .
Pausing by the Bus Eireann bus park
We give them the up yours
Of we will be in Dublin before you.
The defunct engine driver
 Has become a button presser
Gone plump with no coal to shovel.
We bid "arriva derci "to Renmore
As we skirt Oranmore heading east
Through the fields of Athenry
With the hooter pronouncing our immanent
approach
Traversing flooded fields of disgruntled sheep,
Cattle and queuing car drivers at
Flashing level crossings.
White sky lines shadow remote
Clusters of leafless trees
While the occasional dense woodland
Suggests nature is in hiding
As we rock gently through Woodlawn.
Having crossed the lordly Shannon
The oak trees seem one third taller
As deep peaty land nourish from deep down
It seems as tall trees would have deep roots.

While in Clara we stop to idle and ponder
But really to let the Limerick train get through.
Misty foggy midland drizzle douse
And dim my hopeful expectations
Of a sunshine day in the Capital.
Now in Tullamore the barley stubble
Remains unploughed oblivious of
Frosty cleansing healing available
Without chemical insecticides
A dense laziness dawdles in the dew.
We leave cemetery and souls therein beside the track
As we speed towards the spire outside
Portarlington.
The stationmaster there whistles our departure
By the well tended and harrowed fields
As the Dublin man behind airs his accent
Sensing his proximity to the Pale
As he journeys back from the sticks.

Alarm Clack

When one encounters the high-heeled clack
Staccato'd into a bully stomp for attention
You know there is no hope
Of harmony, peace or stillness
Until you have lain like a serpent
Supine and repentant for something
You know absolutely nothing about.
The whim of the whimsical
You are at the mercy of Kali
When female indignation is released
Without conscience, logic, equanimity,
Fair play or justice
But purely on the internal ramblings
Of imagination in the emotional mind
Of someone in anxiety mode.
Impossible to fathom
An invitation to divisive derision and
Despair in the immanent future.

One of those evenings in Mars.

Siesta On Father's Day

After lunch on a sunny Sunday afternoon
A gentle rustling in the leaves
Balms the senses with a breeze.
'Seems half the neighbors are fast asleep
And with the other half there is not a peep
Except now and then
A smack of a ball against a wall
From a little lad about three feet tall,
Whose parents sent him out to play
So mammy and daddy could have their way
Of making Sabbath into something
That put and end to adults grumping.

Spain, 2009.

A Mayfly

Who looks out from within to day

Is it Mr. Sophisticated Scriber Scribbler?

Or Peasant Paddy garden grubber?

Or Histrionic Bemuser of yesteryear?

Or maybe the great lover who has maidens

Restlessly squirming and sighing for the want of him ?

Or perhaps the recipient of relentless resentments

From a passed over power pragmatist?

Yes someone's within, who is content

At times, and fully satisfied at other times,

And glad to be whom he is always.

Yet, still at times, the praise angler

Is still dapping, seeking recognition,

He never matures – it seems.

And I'm here

And I'm still here,

Wondering why?

Why, why, why, and what have

I got to do now?

Am I obligated ?

To someone ?

Anyone ?

Or am I free'

To breathe without owing?

Makes you think doesn't it!

To be in debt from the beginning,

Being born with a resentment –

A terrorist under construction,

A rebellious anarchist has to materialise,

If he is not a cowardly shit.

If the underlying feeling is obligation,

You are a prisoner of sorts

And your jailer the silent recipient

Of your obligation!!!

Am I nice and cosy cuddling my jailer?

Being grateful to a state that enslaved my freedom?!

Should I limp through life?

Doffing my forelock to the German state

Who sheltered and propped our so called Irish Banks

For guarantees individually shouldered , shared per capita.?

A form of TREASON has prevailed

Behind the cloak of government.

In tiger stripes of black and gold,

A usurer's chain mail pyjamas.

In off shore gatherings they guffawed

Jeering as news came thru of banks not going under,

So back for more they have come again to rape

The poor and plunder.

So plunder asunder this country they will do

Shylocked to bankers, tribunaled to who!

The white collar criminal has a grin a mile wide

Enslaving your children is all in his stride.

Voting day 29th, May, 2012.

A Great Life if you Don't Weaken

To ease the pain
From that domain
Wherein this living being dreadeth
To abide or glide and meet the tide
And be up to check "sincero"
To know full well
I met the swell
Yet had not answered with full measure
Disdain the brain
That makes insane the torment of a never.
The "nevers" I had swore once more
That oughtn't be uttered
I asked again for relief to pen,
Plot escape from my predicament.
Ah yes! Stretched taut upon a rack
Of standard stretchers –
Yardsticks for the "paternosters" of our brothers
Endurance limits for the birth pangs of our
mothers.
Chemical disdain for pain, a predicament in
The pharmacy for the infant!?
A breathing place of naturalness,
Where life goes on a breath at a time
Ever changing ever new,
Where with momentum and memory
Hope dawns on the horizon

That the pain will lessen.
A glimmer of light in the darkness of night
Is the tenuous trail I still travel,
Along with my fears, my tears and my years
Of torturous torment and tremors,
I travel alone on the journey home,
And think of the man with the knife in his back,
Who grins in grimaces saying,
"It only hurts when I laugh"
And if I laugh then,
Without remembrance of past pain,
Denial will dawn again, jingling memory bells
While swirling intentions insanely down the
drain.

Commissioned

Commissioned to breathe,
To breathe in and out,
        Without abandon,
 To live.
Commissioned to breathe
 In and out
        With love and care
To live again
And dance the mudra of gratitude
In the reflection of joy in another's eyes.
To swell with fulfillment
 Like the ocean at full tide,
As I gaze at my son,
 With humility and pride,
Delighted,
And lit by the urge to succeed
 And divide
And dissolve.
Kovalam, India, 21/01/05.

Out The Back Window

The mauve yellow blotout mist has moved,
Has moved across between the half leaf shed ash
tree
And the mountain,
While the sky is now less freckled white
But much more blue
With bright sun shining through.
The outline of the mountain is now
Barely visible and seems much further away
And somewhat more inviting for an adventure.
This mist has silenced the bawling cattle
And now just the odd jackdaw wings by,
Not high, but low,
While an eerie static,
Like, like a spasmodic tinnitus
Is perceptible visually and audibly
And glistens in unison and harmony
With the sparkling dew covered retags.
The mist has now departed
Leaving some wispy clouds scudding
northwards
While the sky has cleared to bright blue
Intent on tricking you into a belief,
A belief of permanence for an hour or so,
But I've been caught before,
Without a coat
In the pouring rain.

Entwined 2005 Lá' Le Bríde + 2013 Lá' Le Bríde

An eternal link of eight and on and on,
A welcome day to the first of Spring here in
"God's own country", Kerala.
Welcome back to my sense of smell!
A rose scented joss stick has been lit somewhere
nearby and is wafting it's way
On the light airs with the subtle scent of a puri
frying,
Blended with the herbs used in the morning
samba.
All make their way through my nostrils
And permeate the inner sanctum of my
memoried mind,
Bringing me back, way back before I ever had
this body,
This body that I am now wearing.
Mr. Crow peeks out and takes his palm branch
promenade strutting,
Strutting to a halfway point before his about
turn,
To his shelter cluster of coconuts.
Slim and trim he is with thin Indian legs
And a cheeky regard for humans.
The sun is stretching it's rays

Lighting up the outer reaches of the balcony,
As the sea eagles circle slowly and majestically
In rhythmic unison, surveying the earth-bound gatherers
With a lofty disdain, it seems, or maybe
That's how it would be for me,
If I had the eyes to see like that fish hawk.
To be lean and high flying,
Ethereally buoyant with pranic thrill,

No delay in thought to action
For when you stop, it is to kill.
To halt time for one brief second,
A pause, a brief inhalation for transmogrification to occur
And devour with duty and devotion, drawing deeply
While still fresh, each oxygenated *pranic
particle for purest power.
Life goes on and flies again
Pumping new blood behind the retinas of the preying Mantis eyes.
Now here we are again on the octal Spring
Looped eternally linked by water and common convolvulus,
Ialus as gaeilge, revered by the bean feasa
"Biddy Early".
Revered in Bihar in the vicinity of Buddha's cave,
And in Kerala, the home of Ayurveda the natural medicine,
Known with the exalted title "Vishnughandi" the brain tonic,

The memory stimulant, the ability to recall,
Ah! Yes, known also as Morning Glory, having
hallucinogenic properties,
Now here it is in my own back garden creeping
voraciously among
The culinary herbs of thyme, marjoram, chives,
seeking domination
In it's avaricious appetite for an abundance of
luminescence.
Known as "Bindweed " a scourge.
To know we are all connected,
We are one, entwined back to energy before
matter.

pranic : imbued with life force

1st. February , 2005 & 2013.

Shooeing the Breeze

The breeze that's rustling in the trees
Soft soothing sheeing sounds
That cool the armpits
And sweat oxter hairs.
Butter flies and dragon flies
It bears aloft
And with multitudinous feathery seeds
A part of nature's transports needs
In swishing service sowing.
I ask cool breeze to carry please
A gentle aspiration.
That birds can fly
Free in the sky
Away from man's annihilation
And malpractice manipulation.
In these days of dust and sprays
And new fangled ways
From bi-focaled theory farmers,
Greed intensive
Nature's Kali
On offensive.
Please spare a thought
For natures ways
Where everything was created
And life's not masturbated.
Sweet balming breeze
I ask you please
Blow some sense and sensitivity
Thru Multi National Productivity.

Cahir of Golden Veil

The town of Cahir has come alive,
Pretty girls in light cotton pinks,
Young punkish lads with cocky charm
Summer jollity alive on streets.
The barracks castle once a place of gloom
Now alive with hitchers packs, tourist's maps,
And a lone swan drifting, like in a swoon
Towards a snow white frothing weir
Her head tucked comfy beneath her wing
Surrendered beauty on the Suir-Aisling.
Two youngsters thread their fishing lines
Three lads have gathered to admire the touch
Or offer expert their advice quite free of charge.
Middle aged Deutscher with steifel paunch
In check sports shirt and khaki slacks
Spread out on bench in hobo decadence,
The Teuton factory is far away
And he's relaxed on holiday.
Some well -heeled mothers
With their job now done
In summer fashions to greet the sun
Have stressed with makeup beneath the eyes
To add a twinkle or mask the guise
Of a smouldering daring like corset free,
Shades of Latin love and liberty.
A housewife with her child by hand
Her nipples proud through T- shirt stand
She smiles with open gaiety
And looks you in the eye to see
If you like her are feeling free,
And as for me I'd make her tea.
A convoy of trucks rumble through the town

Earthquaking the pavement they trundle down
A klaxon hoots to show the joy
Perceived by driver still a boy
On his way to Cork with his dinky toy.
A coffee shop called the "Crock of Gold"
Stands beside the bridge – it's new it's old
A serving teenage girl of budding charm
Would tempt a lad to chance his arm
To ask for second portion,
Or on her back to spread tan lotion.

Gay Twenties Air prevail in Cahir
A joy to all who love to share
The warm effects of sunshine.

Lazy observations on a warm summer lunch
time in 1983

My Little Black Bird

Would I like to build a nest with her?
My little black bird.
With her dainty little prance,
Her swirling little glance,
Her hip hop curl the head little dance.
Could I sit beside her on a branch?
My little black bird.
Would my wing extend to shelter her?
"as Gaeilge", could I converse with her?
Warbling music might I romance with her?
With her dainty little prance,
Her swirling little glance,
Her hip hop curl the head little dance..
She has enthralled me you know!
My little black bird.
Could I soar on high and pierce the sky
With pure passion and intention,
And pranam before "*Ganapati's" door
In supplication for reinvention?
With her dainty little prance,
With her swirling little glance,
Her hip hop curl the head little dance,
Could I protect her through the darkest hours?
My little black bird.
Flying gently sipping nectar from the flowers
Could the lovely taste of paradise be ours?
I wonder and wander and wonder?
With her dainty little prance,

Her swirling little glance,
Her hip hop curl the head little dance.
Could we fly away and come back someday?
My little black bird,
Have fresh adventures in some tropical place?
Restart the play embracing grace?
In freedoms realm
On a chirpy note?
With her dainty little prance,
Her swirling little glance,
Her hip hop curl the head little dance..

*Ganapati : Ganesh the son of Siva.

Snide Remarks

Is it possible to get clear of the snide remark?
Without it hurting?
Some day maybe,
 I will be so thick skinned
That it will not penetrate my consciousness
will I be better off that way
more obtuse gnarled and knobbly
With an outer bark that can endure harsh
weather?
 The derisory dermis situated on the periphery
of the touchy feeler antenna
that hovers in expectation alert
and ready for reaction,
not to breathe into it is the key
I suppose.
Well its hard being perfect ,
Isn't it!!

Dogshite Drivel

The doleful doldrums are patiently pacified
By ex pat strollers parading their pets
Among the weeds and litter in Dogshite Park
The poodles who piddle, the wheatens who
widdle
The terriers who tarry and trail their thread
worms
A doberman dumps,a sheepdog shites
Ah its nature on parade for pekinese poohs
The four-legged people exercisers are abundant
Here in Espagne and with present proliferation
Of Chinese Wok Buffets it's great to have an
outlet
For the exotic and unusual.
When you see jockey caps on over fifties
With designer shades masking medication
On retractable lead strollers
Whose yap yaps talk for the dummied owners!

I settle back on my balcony to snooze and
slumber
And ponder and wonder at my inconsequential
observances.

11/3/09.

Sometimes

In the wee small hours of the morning,
While the whole world sleeps,
And I, only me, me alone,
Am the only one awake.
A unique precious feeling of early childhood
Steals over me, and I feel special.
A humming purr from the refrigerator,
Commands the ear for a short spell,
And that, to end in a shudder, then silence,
Until a light spatter of raindrops,
Aquaints me of weather without.
Distraction lurks to lull and lure me
From checking out what lays awaiting me
within.
Within, within, within.
Meaningful meanings of peace and contentment,

That is, when I detach from my insatiable wants.
Those wants,
That queue quietly incessantly for prompt
attention.
My shadow shrouds my shimmer,
This luminescence from within
Wherein I dwell and seek refuge from the world,
And abide by the generosity of each breath.

May 2010.

Starlings

Starlings swinging, swaying,
Clinging, to the nude so bare ash tree,
At the mercy of the remorseless
Waves of westerly winds.
Winds that cull and clear attaching tendrils
And loose bracken that smothered or shadowed
Spring, summer and autumn growth.
Their claws claw, locked firmly
With no dissipation of energy,
As they watch dispassionately
Feeling collectively safer in species unison
Subconsciously surrendered to the force
That binds them,
That continues to caretake them.
Those Ariel devotees that swarm
In the aura of godless nature
Carry a figment of my spirit with them
In their survival adventures over the coming
winter,
As I now watch in cosseted slumber down
Pillow propped and breakfasted,
Awaiting the noon time angelus alarm
On this holiday morning
Wondering
Will I walk the beach, before, or after lunch?

3rd. September 2012.

This Obsession

This obsession that continues to propel and
drive me
This obsession that undermines my longing to
rest,
This obsession that calls for yet another hour of
labour
This obsession that is timeless, restless,
relentless,
This obsession that I so readily embrace and
secretly cherish.
Yes I have a reluctance to reveal this silent
craving,
An ultimate crave for the grave you might say,
Considering its digging, turning, sifting,
weeding the clay,
The soil, the earth, the sand, the stone, the bone,
Our eventual material body destiny.

Yes I persist in the hope of creating pathways to
Places where paradise can be palmed,
Felt unerringly effortlessly intuitively with
certainty and innate contentment.
Contentment that a smiling infant betrays
openly without guile or intent,
Where bees hum in orchestral harmony

Enthralling the silence with thrilling celestial melodies.
Still here I am still lorrying and worrying
Am I born just to be mad.!

Sunday Afternoon on Lighthouse Beach

Another scorcher, back from Ariya Nivas,
vegetarian hotel,
Where I had four iddlys, two puri masalas, and
two chai
All for 105 rupees -less than two euros
Shur, where would you beat that for value.
Sheeba haunts so gently
Smiling her quiet smile
Drinking me with those big eyes
While her big white teeth make up for
 The absence in my mouth.
Its Sunday afternoon, the sun scorches.
The extra locals swell the beach strollers,
Teenage boys ogle the bare western pale flesh
With a lurking suspicion, that it may really be
Forbidden fruit.
So they clasp one another's hands, and squeeze,
And crinkle their new upper lip growth
As they share a giggle.
Ireland seems so far away and so unreal,
Like a land I dreamed of so long ago.
Here in India I am today and
Now is what I have and no more,
It forces me to accept the reality of transience.
A cocky European western strut fools nobody
here
As what goes up must come down.
Change is the constant,

Growth in the heat,
Stretch towards the sun
The coconuts are up there
The shade is cool
But you take your chance
If a coconut falls.
Drains and sewers and rubbish abound
And get swallowed up with fast decay.
The caw caw shrill thrill the tweet twea
And hoopie whoop sounds from the aerial choir
Aloft in the palm trees.
While the odd phut phut from the auto
rickshaws,
Transports and transforms the surroundings
With its human cargo.
Could I live here?
I still don't really know!
My pace would need to alter
My patience would have to grow.
Some new habits I would foster
Some old dogs would have to go
A time clock would need new settings
Sleep patterns never sure snatch snooze
When it's too hot in the shade feel secure.
It can be touchy hot and irritable
If one is suffering from the drought
And one is out, and it's hot and scorchy,
Where the ground just burns your feet,
And there is no shade but street, and traffic
And the fumes and honking in the heat.
Heat haze above exhaust thump clump and
clatter.
Red blue magazines and pictures
Hang from clothes pegs on each stall,
Busy beauties smile comuppence

To rise above the grime and take the mind
Away from crime and time
Hangs in abeyance to be picked up
At some future date..
While in the meantime one has to be aware
Or it's not there.
What you thought was lost forever
Flashed once again before your eyes
Like the turquoise flash of a flying hummingbird
Stops time when I espy and I sigh with joy
To be the boy, inside this old rag body
With bones, with bones, that are at long last
warm.
Shur a bollix to begrudgers
Aren't I far away from harm.

Sunday 6th February 2005.

The Black Messengers

The black messengers alight
Side by side they observe
Scavengers scanning the savages.
They know, they have witnessed,
Witnessed our plunder and pillage.
Caw cawing in cacophony,
They smirk mockingly menacingly
At our grounded ineptitude
Our inability to husband this planet
With any degree of heartfelt gratitude.
Ok, so they await rebirth in human form
Again having been relegated,
Yet they are in no hurry to join
The present generation of parasitic plodders
In their destruction of this pleading planet.
*Thanaig an Fiach dubh
Chun na súile a tharraingt as Cuchullain
Roimh eitilt a anam as a chorp.*
Me doubts they will come
For any modern western souls
In the northern hemisphere.
Would you if you could wing
Away from this pollution?

*the raven came to extract *Cuchullain*'s eyes
before his soul left his body*.

On the Steps of the Court House

On the steps of the court house,
I sit and await justice and resolution.
Am tired and weary of loneliness and
uncertainty
While the masquerading victim vulture preys for
more.
Varanasi tinkles a beckoning bell,
The Ganges flows,
The lotus candles run towards the ocean
A spark of my own light adjoins them
And when my time comes
I shan't beg to tarry.
The children were worth this stay on earth
Every breath a gift when not attached to *maya.
Stressed manipulators of facts and figures clack
heels
On polished tiled floors where the high ceilings
of Colonial buildings
Echo and ring the gongs of haunted hopes.
Unvoiced aspirations linger and loiter and
huddle
Before the "call over".
An air of expectancy trundles thru the aisles and
benches

Of the courtroom -marking time.
Monosyllabic muttering and acquiesces of
nodding affirmatives
Suggest progress.
All stand again as the judge heads for chambers.

*maya (illusion)

Who is beating the drum today?

Who is beating the drum today?
The question lingers-
It has its way
Of putting my mind
In the dunce's corner
Of reluctance to say.
Who is the leader at the forefront
Of my hopes and desires
Who is trembling me awake
In the prime rays of morning
Who in my heart do I wish to impress
Is there any one out there
That's causing me stress
Time is unwinding,
Spring coil is slackening.
Does the flute play the master
Or does the master play the flute.

June 09 Torrevieja.

Glad of a Trolley in A&E

Being backed up on a trolley in Accident and
Emergency Galway,

At last I feel somewhat saner,

Pain, delirium, and high fever abated,

I'm hopeful of some tea and toast,

Having tasted naught for three days now.

My head knots up in twisted thoughts

Of the last two nights, and my unhinged

And constant perambulating mind.

That hamster wheel that whirled me round,

Spun a spell on the edge of hell,

Where no rest came, until Dr. Sammy

From Northern Borneo shone his gentle

Intelligence and kind probing, to ease

The situation with a listening ear,

And prompt action.

I thank you forest man! And wish you

Joy in your endeavours on your one acre

Way down under.

A great soul, I know you are!   Wild Man.

28/12/2011

Watching The Road

The north wind blows cold,
Remnants of snow remain to remind me
Of chores to be done in light,
Before it's night and cold again.
The rose hips red stand clear
Of the rusty scrawbing briar,
Reminding me of the pain in ageing beauty.

The cold wind blows
'Tis I that pass and time remains.
Nicholas, bent, went by upon his cycle
The restless muttering of the mind
Transferred itself to the feet and propelled
The pedals down the hill to the well
Of oblivion.

Sunday morning, December 9th 1990

My Sympathies

In a church on the border,
The leaders assembled to feed,
Their collective selective facility to breed
A genetically modified mongrel of greed.
They would profit *mar dhea,
The poor in society, the gullible, the inane,
The media suckling bonamhs,
The tabloid sensationalists and serial sitcom
followers.
Yes, gobshite Paddy would swallow and follow
The wanker banker, the insurance broker,
The multinational pharmaceutical Chairmen
The Agri Fertilizer Bossmen, the Insecticider
Sanitizer,
Boosted of course by the Advertising Spinners
And the *plámás men in Public Relations.
Such a conglomeration of parasite predators had
of course
In train their camp followers of barristers,
government ministers,
Bishops, Bailiffs, Judges, Tobacco and Distillery
Executives.
"A Fracking Breakthrough was the Lure",
To cure the ills of a fluttering economy
And stir the stagnant marketplace
Of irresponsible, irreprehensible, trading
And resurrect the growling pussy, who wanted
more,
So to score they had come along the selective
grapevine.

"All who have entered this hallowed domain
Have signed in with their signatures online
On screen and can be seen and witnessed
By their neighbour of clout – there's no doubt
Making sure of veracity of all they might say or
sign away.
The security on the door was made sure".
All doors were locked now steel barred and
secure
What transpires within here will forever insure
your place
In the Annals of Ireland's Impure Manure
With what you are about to endure.
I am here in the pulpit packed full with TNT,
Your Shepherd today, sheep shearing will
follow,
You all have to pay for past sins of the mortal
Where you fleeced the flock, and once again

You planned to FRACK the sod of Eireann
Where our forefathers shed their blood
And where you had planned to flood
Our clean waters with toxic chemicals
Lead , Uranium, Mercury, Ethylene Glycol,
Formaldhyde, HCL, and Radium all carcinogens
and
Other waste materials from the dumps and
cover ups
In your inefficient waste disposal units
And those GM products that went so wrong.
Oh! Yes I know you all are contrite
And I insured you'd make amends
That's why I got you all to sign away
Your property, goods and chattels,

With your witnessed signatures on the online wills
And your collective pact in this mass suicide,
For as you see my right finger is on the button,
When it's removed we all ascend,
So "MY Sympathies" to your offspring
They will fare better in the end.
So we will all bless ourselves,
In the Nam---.

*allegedly= mar dhea   *flattery= plámás

The Spirit of Tipperary

Ag tosnu. Gooldscross to Limerick Junction. A tricky route with briars and fairy thorn to *scraube* one if one should veer or hunt along the way. The Suir river flows through Ardmayle, under the bridge by the Creamery, where the clanging of churns still echo the morning stillness, as horses whinny, chains clack, and iron shod wooden wheels crunch and splinter pebbles on the roadside. Boherlan had beaten Clonulty was to be heard in guffaw in the time warp. Dragonflies were in abundance and mayflies were no doubt about. And although it was crisp 'twas clear summer was on the way. Expectancy hovered in consciousness, time stood still, very still. Maia, the daughter of Atlas and mother of Mercury by Jupiter, a merry month when young people wash their faces in the May morning dew and thereby refresh their vigour. And somehow I stood on the wall of the bridge observing the hurly burly of a Monday morning, where men bartered with cabbage plants, seed potatoes and some penknife shavings from a plug of Mick McQuaid or Old Condor, or a little sup of the creathur to take the sting out of the morning and clear the vision for the day ahead.

The camaraderie of working men accustomed to hardship, pain, endurance, and used to toiling in the most inclement weather, was heartening to behold and lifted my hopes. The backbone of rural Ireland was in evidence here before me and not the imagery presented by the slick mouthpieces of political parties or vested interests of big business fronted by upholders of the Bar and Kings Inns or the softened piranha pulpit preachers. It's hard to beat the clarity that is clearly perceptible thru the mist and steamy fog that rises up from hard-working dray horses on a frosty morning and the mingled sniff of sweat from man and animal united in labour. Real communion is where truth abides and true communism begins to replace the fearful paranoid selfish submission to the abdication of responsible parenting. Here I am still standing on the bridge in my short trousers, chilblained thighs, and scabby, bruised knees with a question mark of black curly hair hanging over the squinting eye of doubt and growing skepticism. *Credo, Credo*, is only **cré* in the long-run. We all go back to it, just like the Suir in a yellow flood after heavy rain up stream near the Devil's Bit on the way to the sea. And if we sidetrack this 'yellow flood' to a stagnant pool with no current, it settles into just clay, the minerals from whence we came and with water and light began. Le solas De. "Le cúnamhh solas 'gus grá taimse". With the help of light and love I am in body form now, perceptible in spirit form, not quite invisible, but tangible in the notions and daydreams of gypsy fiddlers, bygone harpists, poets and patriots, swami communists and *premies of all ages.. "Alone, all alone by the wave washed strand. All alone in Slieve na mBan".With a dream of love in the core of your heart, your heart, you are indestructible, you live forever. In such a state of grace abides a vision of a fountain, a well that provided sustenance to man, beast and crops subterraneously linked to Aherlow River and then eventually to the Suir, flowing, flowing, flowing. This journey is what it is about, the destination is destitution - if we should stop and become attached, we continue going on, going on, growing beyond dimensions of big or small, good or bad, beautiful or ugly for this wonderful gift of life and the capacity and opportunity it grants with each breath to feel within and be the creator of love. Yes, a great omnipotent feeling full to the brim of good will, with not the slightest space for negativity. To realise such experience with its depth and profundity was difficult for the boy on the bridge, surrounded as he was by the family and cultural circumstances he was born into, or maybe had chosen to be born into. To realize! is why he got a body and a life, to make real, to bring certainty, to verify by experience his own true nature. Who am I? Not the powerless infant who had water poured on his head by a celibate and had brandy and champagne foisted on his undeveloped metabolism by an unconscious or unaware grandfather in so-called celebration of the perpetuity of a name continuing to run from his blood lines. No the attempt to shackle him to the flock of sheep who could abdicate their responsibility for selfish actions by mere

confession, to an altar performer of so-called
sacrifice was not acceptable then or now.
"Alone, all alone by the wave washed strand"
No he knew even then from whence he came
and he had no need for confirmation or any
interpreter between him and the source of life
that breathed him. Dogs and birds were sure
companions and had always alerted him to
certainty, the sound in the silence, the light in
the darkness, the companionship in the
wilderness, while his nostrils still flared to
screen and identify each new scent. Close to
nature was safer than civilization. He had seen
the Aurora Borealis and was intrigued and while
going to sleep at night, sailed astral among the
Seven Sisters knowing that snakes and dragons
were part of his past lives here in Munster. In
the day to day world of parents, teachers, and
schools, light was always defined by it's
shadow. So consequently all innocent little
beings kept their light under a bushel or else
they invoked the wrath and punishment from
those who dominated and overwhelmed in the
dark clerical shadow world. Demon-strance
from the monstrance at so-called benediction
time, seemed set up to terrify and overwhelm
the questions by those seeking any increase in
devotional attitude, a sham in the portrayal of a
Real Presence. The Real Presence glows golden
bright and is fanned by each gifted breath,
which every secure infant beholds within him,
or herself, and that is without instruction from
any church, state or authority. Another throw-
back to the bridges at Ardmayle I find myself
galvanized like an empty water bucket awaiting

the gush of water from the third stroke of the pump. My time-warped familiar peers petulantly at me looking upwards from downcast, furrowed, worried, brows and I wonder to myself "what's this past, present and future business". There are times in life when it feels, all the one. "Feeling at one with it all" gives great latitude for expansion and allows me bi-location faculties between the Moat of Ardmayle and that Shiva rock mound in Kerala, when India was known as Argavarta, the abode of the Aryans, (the noble worthy people). The Shi were in evidence here then and still held a strong and meaningful influence on those that lived by the fordable river here. When the river was in flood then, the Criostopher, a simple, kind giant, stood forth to ferry the needy and something of that great strength and kindness still lurks in the vicinity of the bridge that was built on the spot.

The magical properties from downstream are further enhanced as the clumh eala (swan down), clúmh seala (signet down) mingle with the waters of the Clodiagh. The soul paddlers that were happy to continue existence in long-necked form, hollow voicing inward sounds of "hansa" content and serene in acceptance, awaiting, awaiting, awaiting, the dawning.

Yes, time is shown for what it is in the maya mirror - Rush and hurry have not been ushered into consciousness. Like Kristy Sidartha on the banks of the surging river, wondering what he could meaningfully do, he realised – he could sit – he could wait.

Peace, real peace prevails in such realizations-
that is when one is not preoccupied with feeding
family. The seriousness and tension in the air
that depravation provided was grounding and
anchored the bridge to present day
circumstances. (*a hungry refrain swings in
suspension*)
To get the start put you on the way
With camaraderie of working men
Then and only then could the spirit soar
A hope could roar once more
In the vacuumed hollows tunnelled by long
suffering deprivation
To have work with pay
Would brighten the darkest day
And nourish the seed of a future expectation.
"A red flag will eventually flutter".
Ah yes! The tough uncle yank priest praised
"McCarthy" And killed communists in his head
with his monogrammed hunting rifle. He spent
bigshot, loud and hearty. While the other gentle-
voiced uncle yank priest, distributed his dollars
to the poor relations and gave encouragement
towards education and never a word of
condemnation. From the middle of a bridge, it's
a great place to view the world –one foot
towards tomorrow the other one towards
yesterday and what's going beneath you is today
and that's flowing. "Nearly never bulled a cow
"and every country child who had faculties
knows that for sure, but they have the good
sense not to talk too much about it in front of the
adults.

Now I remember the actress from London and Dublin – Rosie and she was gorgeous .She had curly blonde hair and wore see through lace-curtain nightdresses around the farm in the afternoon. And she'd tousle my hair while she was looking at the big black Frisian bull doing his duty. She would sing a lovely dreamy song and laugh when it was over, and then make tea to wash down the Marietta biscuits.

My father always got excited and was always laughing and joking with her and she with him but if my mother heard it "there was who began it" for the best part of a week around the house – oh! She'd be very vexed entirely. Even though she liked Rosie too but she didn't want my father to like her. Adults are quare aren't they?! Well while still on the bridge here looking down stream to the field on the left, the poor black bull is now chained from the nose pulling a railway sleeper around a field to slow him down, while a pile of red heifers are teasing him with their bawling and prancing on top of one another from across the field on the other side of the river. Well now he is the buck that would put *smacht* on them if he got over. Then –loud and clear across the river, the bull, the heifers, and the workmen around the creamery all freeze, to listen, all of them cocking their heads, to the cuckoo-cuckoo-cuckoo.

*cré   clay
*premies   lovers of truth

The Tablecloth

I was at the big table, the smell of moth balls was coming off the banquet cloth, the one with the embroidered motifs of the fleur-de-lis, the funny flower that granddad wore at Easter, the special cloth for important occasions. It was St. Stephen's Day. It was sad, sad mournful, "Anach Cuain,Then "Sliabh na mBan" and then "The Boys from Barr na Sráide" who hunted with the wren, but it wasn't mummer music at all, what with everyone saying sorry for your troubles. Something terrible has happened, I know something terrible has happened, I know and "Sonny the Sniff" my dog he knows too, he is keeping so close! Mamma has been crying, she keeps crying, she holds me so tight but she won't tell me what it is, the smell of mothballs and lavender. I beg her to tell me but she insists that there is nothing for me to worry about. Everything would be all right. "God will look after us, Suiless, Suiless, Suiless".

They took me away that night, off down the country with Ned the foreman driving the cattle truck.   They said it was to Granddad's old home where Auntie Wilmot was going to take care of me.   Now, Auntie Wilmot was granddad's new wife's sister. She was a real fibber and I did not like her.   I don't know what she looked like and neither did Mama know because she never let us touch her face.

Auntie Wilmot and Ned the foreman were not to be trusted and Mama would tell me that with a double tap of her fingers on the back of my hand as that is how we warned one another.   From the time they took me away to Auntie Wilmot to this day, has been dreadful.   I can't remember much. I was given very rough clothes to wear and some old boots that let in water if you walked in a puddle.   Then after a week or so I was brought to a school in the city where they said my name was Seamus Dall, the culchie, an orphan from down the country.

I was to shut up and stop snivelling and do what I was told, when I was told and I would learn something eventually.   My bed was at the top of the stairs in the big dormitory just beside the door where the other boys hid things in my bed that I was to shut up about, or I would get the treatment.   The treatment was terrible.   Your head was held under the water in the washroom until you nearly burst or choked.So to know nothing was to know something important.   My best friend in the school was Whaa Bower who could only hear gentle sounds and no one come to see him either. Whaa played the *bodhrán* and my other friend was Limpy Lumpy who had a club foot and a hunchback.   But could he play the fiddle.   The birds would sit down on the wall, and the lads in the yard would stop fighting just to listen to him.

I found it easy to play most wind instruments,
after a few days I generally got the hang of them
but the uilleann pipes thrilled me most, a one
man orchestra I would feel I was all by myself,
with tones, undertones, melodies, harmonies,
blending pain, sorrow, joy romance, devilment,
ecstasy. You could paint pictures with the pipes,
all you needed was audience and forgiveness.
When the main school band played for the GAA,
We played for the boys who were astray,
And those in borstal, Letterfrack,
And those of us they had to hide
Were locked inside where we had to bide,
Until one day we'd be let away.
That day came.
I had my name
Of Seamus Dall from down the country,
Released we were without a clue
Of what to do
Or where to go
And so
We agreed to stay together.
We formed a band called "The Mystery Boys".
Stella Maris was our home on Spyglass Hill and
we played, sorrowful, joyful and glorious for
funerals, weddings and anniversaries.
Then one day, a booking for a St Stephen's Day,
25th anniversary, we were asked to play for a
big house down the country. Whaa Bower and
Limpy felt the gig was a bit too far away. But it
was a strange request for an awkward day and
we felt it would be different.
Whaa drove the van and we were glad to get
away from Christmas and the city.

Then as we came through an archway at the gatehouse up a long avenue, Limpy told us that he had heard that the woman who had hired us was worth a fortune. She had been locked away too for over twenty years. Demented she'd been after her husband and fathers tragic deaths. Oh it was sad.

Well we were given grand rooms and told to come down to the big table where there was a place for us.

Whaa and Limpy were in great form with a couple of drinks inside them. But for me it was strange and eerie - the feel of the banister, the echo in the hallway, the smell of lavender

The grub was great and it was time to play – anything we liked – it was a memorable day. A few jigs and reels warming up the pipes. Then Limpy wooed them with "The Coolin" Another slow air was then called for. I reached for the pipes and got the most powerful smell of mothballs. Then the feel of the fleur-de-lis tablecloth was familiar. Straightaway without thinking the pipes came out came out with "Anach Cuain" , a cry for "Sliabh na mBan" and that was the ancient version that trembled o. Then "The Boys from Barr na Sráide" flowed in an outburst of pent- up passion and emotion but before it was finished a woman's hands were feeling all over my face and then crying "Suiless, Suiless, my boy, my son. They said you had gone to heaven with the two of them."

The Phantom of the Forgotten Friary

A hoodie figure, more than six feet tall, shrouded in a gaunt shimmer, an aura of bleak frostiness exuding at least two feet out from all his extremities, glided down Friar Street. Some shards of light were barely visible on the horizon over the railway hill. 'Twas like, the dawn was being restricted, restrained from shafting light down through the wisps of mist and fog that clung to some of the doorways and alleyways. A terrier two sheepdogs, and a lurcher, who were all in line to cover a red setter bitch in full heat, all stopped, cowed, halted and whimpered as the figure approached. The morning angelus bells from the Cathedral were more than three minutes late this morning and a silent but stern admonishment permeated the sleeping street inhabitants. They were nearly all asleep, except for the young lad and the auld Fenian, neither slept much, the young lad had an insatiable lust for life and every experience it had to offer.

"Go out to Leahy for a fresh loaf the first batch should be cooling and ask him for a couple of bottles of stout. You go in yourself and get them, in the shed beside the bakery, where he does the corking, and if there is 'ere a baby power knocking about, get that too".
The Fenian had been up late, chewing the fat with Bill the Black and that generally meant they drank gin till sunset, and whiskey thereafter.

Bill the Black had been in jail for his part in the mutiny of the Connaught Rangers 1st. Battalion at Jullundur and Solan in India, had been sentenced to death too, but unlike young Daly, his pal who was executed, he got reprieved due to threatened pressure from strong Fenian sources. Being a little lad, I'd be sent to bed early, and when my parents went themselves to bed, I sometimes snuck out to Carey's snug, where the auld Fenian, my grand uncle, would snigger, and look at me" you couldn't sleep auld stock, could you" and he'd buy me a lemonade and a bag of broken biscuits, where I'd hear songs, yarns, verses of Robert Service, Kipling,and Raftery, *an file*, till near dawn. Now Connie Carey, a character of compassion, had the pub, grocery and bakery. There was a laneway right beside the pub with rooms overhead the lane, and a gate which could be closed, especially at the official pub closing time, giving late drinkers a sense of security with the alternative back exit on to private property. This lane way was an old right of way, and was in existence long before Friar Street became a street and Connie or the Fenian made sure the gate was opened an hour before first light. Twice they forgot and remained drinking in the bar and then looking through the bar window, witnessed the big gates being smashed like matchsticks by the hooded friar who turned to face them with his eyes afire, glowering and his finger raised in stern admonishment.

The second time it happened, Tipperary had won the Munster Final against Cork, the game was played in the town the previous day and celebrations had continued throughout the night into the dawn and this time it was witnessed by a crowd of revelers too, from Mrs.Mullaneys pub opposite. The new gate was smashed, two bicycles crumpled, a horse trap's wheels and shafts torn off by the blazing friar, the horse had bolted and was found two days later in a neighboring county never to go between the shafts again. Father Power the parish priest tried to bless the laneway and the holy water was said to have evaporated in the bowl before the eyes of the altar boys and Power's hair turned from jet black to pure white in under a week. So Power was left with no power was the saying in the town. You don't mess with the fried friar from Friar Street..

dan de dan dan.-- to be continued

The Climb

"A ball of malt, a pint of stout and chai latte like a decent woman and will you have something yourself seeing that it's rarely I am in nowadays, its good to see you Nora "Well Tom it's good to see you and its looking well you are too." Nora put up the drinks on the counter, popped the steam nozzle into the milk jug and through the steam that was rising up, studied Tom's freshly shaved complexion as he chatted to the two men while handing them the drinks. That wild buck had straightened himself out, he gave up the drink, got his last two children through college with master degrees, not so shabby that now" she thought to herself and felt herself smirk inwardly noting that there was spring in him. Nora had had her own troubles over the last four or five years, she had buried her husband Bernard the same week as Tom had buried his wife Kate. She took over the pub, the farm the gambling debts and three wayward teenagers that had been given free rein by an affable, loveable, rogue of an indulgent father.
Tom and Bernard had been good friends, they went on the wagon every Lent, except for their excursion to The Cheltenham Festival and what happened there was their business and no more questions.
 Tramore, Listowel, and Galway race meetings were also annual events for the boys. Kate and herself were expected to step up at these times and take over all duties.

The two women had a week or ten days
sometimes in New York, London or Paris. They
worked hard too and deserved to play as well.
Fair was fair and that was the way it was but
Kate got a brain tumour and was gone in a few
days while Bernard suffered in and out of St.
John of God's getting dried out and then the
liver gave out. They died within days of one
another. In a sort of a way it was a relief to have
Bernard gone as the moodiness with herself and
the children near the end was intolerable, but
she missed him, and she missed her close friend
and confidant Kate. While handing Tom the chai
late the cup and saucer rattled a little as some
unbidden memories flooded in for a moment
and then passed. But Tom noticed and just
stroked the back of her hand with a sensitive
acknowledgement of old friendship. They had
been in primary school together, there had been
birthday parties as children while their parents
and families had always been very close. Nora
bit her lip with a memory of being put in the
bath with Tom as a three or four year old. They
had both gone in to the piggery to see the new
little bonamhs and had fallen in the sloppy
smelly muck, screaming for help, as they were
chased by the enormous sow.
Their parents had laughed as they stripped the
two of them putting them into a warm bath
together and that's where they discovered they
were different. She still remembered his big eyes
looking at her down there. Their eyes met and
held for a moment but the presence of the other
two men in the bar prevented any follow up.

Tom put a spoon of sugar in the chai latte stirred it slowly while Nora poured a little sherry for herself as the three waited for her. They lifted their glasses and Tom his cup, saying "you know this is eerie, like déjà vu". Five years ago Kate was taken into hospital, Bernard had been in for a couple of weeks and was about to be operated on, just the four of us were here all worried, in fact it was the last drink I had". Tom had a tear in the corner of his eye and the boys spotted it saying "you were great Tom to stay off it, look how your life has turned around. *S'hur* yourself and Bernard were devils when ye were on it. Not, mind you, that ye were bad or anything, but ye were yer own worst enemy, would you not agree, Nora"? Nora paused, tilted her head, shook it a little, then while looking into the middle distance, muttering to herself "I said I would climb Everest if those two gave up the drink". She drained her sherry and emphasised with a knock on the counter "and I will do the reek next Wednesday seeing its five years " Well climbing the reek "Croagh Patrick" was regarded as a religious penance, a pronouncement of devotion or and expression of gratitude in Christian terms. They called the mountain itself after St. Patrick, the man who had brought Christianity to Ireland. The mountain was well known to have had healing, sacred, and magical properties by the Druids long before Christianity usurped its prominence, totally ambivalent to its Siva Lingam properties, "mar dhea". Tom looked at the two lads and herself, stood up, put out his hand to Nora and said "I will do it with you, I'll call for you at ten". Nora had togged out for the reek in her own inimitable way, a tartan kilt, a pair of Doc Martin boot, woolly socks, an off white Aran sweater with the sheep oil retained in the wool to ward off the mist that might be encountered, a pair of tasty panties for auld decency and devilment for the chaser, a four foot staff, a loan of her daughters I Phone with head phones and a bottle of Lucozade for the thirst and the energy. She said to herself "I'll stiffen St. Patrick himself if he is still around". She got out of the passenger seat revealing to Tom a lovely white thigh that flashed memories of past paradises before his startled stagger. Tom shook his head like a drenched cocker spaniel coming out of a freezing river to clear his vision as it were and smirked his boldest smile at Nora who shook out her long red hair at him laughingly saying" I'll beat you to the top" and I'll see can you live up to your name, Tomás Mac Tire, Woof Woof." (*mactíre* being the gaelic for wolf) Off she went at a brisk trot. Tom grabbed his length of hazel, and his bottle of water, his Munster rugby supporter's anorak, and set off after her with his heart pounding, not having been this excited since Ireland beat England in Croke Park, at the rugby. "Oh Lord above 'tis mighty "he said to himself as he felt the yen coming on him as well. If this was what climbing Croke Patrick was about, there wouldn't be room to move on the mountain, and here now, they had it all to themselves, so they better make the most of it. Nora had stopped to put on the head phones with the Beatles up loud , "All you need is love, love is all you need, love,

love, love, love, is all you need," like a mantra inside her, trembling her body it was, she couldn't stop it and she didn't want to stop it. As she climbed her excitement mounting with all this exercising and stretching her body to the extremes, it was carrying her back to her early twenties. Her mind was afire and she was light and carefree one second and the next she was about to become an old woman. She paused for more air but also to reflect and embrace these energised feelings that coursed raw animal lustful longings in her loins. Noticing that the waist band of her kilt had moved up from the hips to over the belly button where it definitely felt more comfortable, modesty was prompting her to pull it down, but devilment stayed her hand. She noticed Tom panting and puffing up the slope some thirty feet behind her with a big red turkey face on him like her late husband used to have with a couple of Viagra and a *bodán* that would beat an ass out of a sandpit. She roared laughing, a mocking laughter directed at Tom" you'll have to hurry if you want to beat me ", and after a little pause giggling "with that yoke "and she started to howl again with laughter. Tom nearly tripped, toppled a little then recovered which startled Nora for a moment and then they both started to laugh like two big kids and he after her. They were more than half way up they paused in the climb to look around down into Clew Bay which was magnificent. Grace O' Máile, the Pirate Queen, who had sailed out from there and up the Thames Estuary showing bottle to the English that had never been shown before or since. Her heart swelled up with pride and with renewed vigour she set out for the summit. While she was stopped Tom was gaining on her, he too stopped to admire, but not the scenery, but the lovely figure with the long legs and red hair and the exuding sensuality that was fit to break down any human. He thought of their late spouses Kate and Bernard and contemplating for a moment, relished in the encouragement he was certain of from the both of them. So with that clarity his heart skipped and he knew his intentions were wild but honourable. Nora saw the change in him, bit her lip and thought to herself "I'm a slut". "No I'm not, but he will have to catch me". They were both breathing hard and as they neared the top it got harder. The stones scattered under their feet and with the mist coming down it was slippery and dangerous enough. Now the only sound was rocks scattering and heavy breathing and it seemed to echo around them. Suddenly it darkened with a fall in temperature, a cloud burst with very heavy hail and what had been heavenly was suddenly hostile. A rush was called for to the little white chapel on the hill and the cry of pain from Nora as she skidded on a stone brought the hibernated Munster rugby forward back into play as chief protector. Within seconds he had Nora over his shoulder in a fireman's hold with his big boots pounding and large stones scattering under the determination to reach shelter. They reached the door of the chapel to find it locked against them and as Tom slid Nora down against the door asking "is it bad" and she still with her arms around him looking into his eyes says "it couldn't be better." The body heat was steamy and the hail shower was passing, the church door was rattling to a steady rhythm as Tom said "I'd climb up here every day for this" and you won't need the church's approval either as far as I'm concerned said Nora laughing in her last clutching spasm. Then they both started to hum and sway into one another to an old Bob Dylan number "Knock Knock Knocking on Heaven's Door".

Fish

Fish deprivation, lent, one full meal and two collations, oily sardines, tinned salmon, (An Bradán Feasa, Fionn Mac Cumhal).

I was eight years old from an inland town and had just come with my parents and little brother to live out the country. It was very exciting for me;   full of adventure opportunities as we would be living in a very, very big house with a long avenue, a high walled orchard, big trees, right beside a river and a lake. We were going to be living here for a couple of years while my father, who was a teacher, would build our new house after school hours, at the edge of the town. My new friend Mossie loved to go fishing and he brought me with him. I was instantly hooked and wanted a fishing rod too. His father Paddy Joe saw my predicament, offered me a machete, brought me to a sally grove, outlined the tallest straightest sally rod and let me hack it down, to be trimmed to a ten foot length.   I was given about sixteen feet of brown fishing line, a foot of cat gut,   a black hook. Mossie showed me the tricky knots especially with the cat gut and how to set it all up. I had to do it all by myself, that was part of the fun. Getting the big long juicy worms, digging them out of the dung heap and keeping them in a jam jar.

Then to prod the worm into the head with the hook and slide him right up it, so the eels, the trout or the perch couldn't see the hook. There still was more to be done, a cork had to be cut half way through it, then a little piece of lead the size of your finger nail you overlapped on the cat gut and bit into it so that it gripped and didn't fall off. The excitement you can't imagine and then the cork had to be slid onto the line where it had been cut and placed about two feet above the cat gut. Then to get it into the water, in the deep part where the water looked black and wasn't moving much. You waited and watched the cork. How many hours I watched the cork I don't remember but the sounds and sights, the ripples and flights of birds, insects, mayflies, dragon flies, water hens, kingfishers, otters, wild ducks and the graceful swans, were not wasted on the little town boy. One jar of worms later, one twelve inch and one sixteen inch eel were my proud trophies and were still wriggling as I presented them to mamma. I can still hear her screaming at me to get them out of the house immediately. The dogs watched me carefully with their heads moving inquiringly from side to side as I washed them under a tap in the back yard, having slit them with my penknife under the throat, chopped of their heads and pulled out their guts and they were still wriggling every so often.

Getting the skin off was hard, I needed help,
Mossie held and I pulled. I chopped them up
and cooked them on a frying pan over the hot
coals of an open fire in Mossie's mother's house.
The eels were very oily but nicer than sardines
and I kept a few pieces wrapped up in a
newspaper for my father when he came home.
He liked them. My little brother didn't like
them, he was too small. I went on to make a
three piece rod from bamboo canes joined up by
copper ferrules (made up from left over
plumbing pieces from the new house my father
was building after school hours). It took me
nearly a whole day to cut the copper with the
blunt hack saw blade I had. Then I had to make
the eyes to run the line through and that was
another day. I curled pieces of wire along a
poker stretching them out a little bit leaving
about three quarters of an inch on each side
which had to be flattened out a little with a
hammer so it could be tied flatly on to the cane.
To tie the eyes to the cane properly required a lot
of work. I had to go to a shoemaker and get
some hemp and a ball of wax from him. You
then got about four lines of hemp a little over
two feet long and tied a knot at both ends, then
you warmed the wax with your hands and when
it started to soften you pulled the hemp through
it ten or twenty times so it looked like single
black string that was slightly sticky. With this
you tied the rings to the cane so the string
looked really like a professional one piece glued
up job. I got a wooden reel from Mossie's father
with heavy green line at least twenty pound
breaking strain that had to be soaked in linseed

oil and I was nearly ready for the big time. I had
a light silver English tanner burning a hole in my
pocket and couldn't wait to get into Kilroy's
where they sold all the fishing gear. I got twelve
black hooks suitable for eels, perch, trout and
night lines for a penny, two triple hooks for
another penny, and then some tracing wire,
catgut, a few split rings and a few swivels for the
four pence that was left. Excitement like this
put Santa Claus in the halfpenny place. I was
nine at this stage and could tell you long stories
about the ones that got away. On a yellow
flood, that was after very, very heavy rain you
could get an odd trout with a worm perch and
eels no trouble but at the weekends Mossie's
father would let us go for pike. Now pike –
frightening, fighting fish, with razor sharp teeth
that ran backwards, where you could loose your
finger and be pulled into the river. They bashed
the water and you had to tire them by letting
them in and out, your finger got burned with the
line on a big one. Now to catch one, you stuck
the tracing wire with a triple hook on the end of
it up a frogs hole and out his mouth, a loop on
the tracing attached to the heavy line, you
whirled him in to the deep end where the pikes
were known to lurk. The frog would swim
like mad and then snap and you'd stop
breathing cause your reel would go spinning
and everything was dangerous and you had to
get calm steady and quiet. I will never forget the
first few and then the real big one, nearly as long
as myself, and that nearly drowned me, while I
was bawling crying but would not let go and
kept playing him. Getting him to the bank took

nearly twenty minutes, where Mossie's father
Paddy Joe stuck the gaff in behind his gills and
hauled him up on the bank, well up 'cause he
was still leaping. He had to be hammered on the
head full force with the handle of the gaff to kill
him. Now that was a real fish. To keep him up
off the ground with my fingers in his gills I
needed one hand to help the other. Mossie, in
later life became the wild life bailiff and warden
and a conservationist for that same stretch of the
river Suir and gave classes at one stage to the
IRA prisoners on how to make and tie flies for
fly fishing and was known as a gold medal
winner in the Chelsea flower show for his prize
Sweet Peas, and Dahlias. He was a great lover of
all wildlife and I hope we meet again in the next
life.

Lady's Well

The sun is splitting the rocks, mother is touchy irritable, father is gone off playing golf as usual, my jobs are done and the garden weeded. I told my friend Cuddy that I would meet him in Lady's Well, if I was let. "Mamma I want to meet my friend down the road ". "You're not going anywhere without your little brother, you bring him with you " "Ok!" I shout upstairs and hurry as I think she is going out herself - titivating herself upstairs! I got my togs and towel on the carrier and got the little fellow up on the cross bar and was gone before you can say " Jack Robinson ".   We are singing now as I pedal to "There's a Pawn Shop round the corner in Pittsburgh Pennsylvania ".   We are off to Lady's Well on the other side of town. Up over the railway bridge puffing and panting, whizzing down to the right along Butler Avenue avoiding my grandmother's house and away out the watery mall. Up past McGrath's Cinema. Way out the golf links road and just over the bridge at Turtilla I turn down by the river. I am sweating, breathing hard but delighted to be away. The little fellow is complaining of having a sore backside with pins and needles in one leg from sitting on the bar of the bike but he is happy and excited too. We are having an adventure. I wheel the bike along the bank of the river. I explain to him that this is where I come to when I go fishing.

We look out on the river, where the big trees
reach well out and dip into the water and gather
scum, hay, straw and little twigs. Underneath in
the long green weeds there I tell him that that's
where the big pike live, hiding, waiting to jump
out and catch and gobble up the minnows, the
dearogs when the current makes them pass by.
He wanted to go closer to look and I had to grab
him and explain that it was deep there; that the
bank was steep, and the very edge underneath it
can be eaten by the fast river, so if you stepped
on it, it might give way, and you could drown.
He loved looking at the water flickering light
through the leaves and we listened to the sound
the water made flowing over the stones. The
buzzing noises and insect life, horse flies,
mayflies, dragon flies, butterflies and the odd
water hen skittering on the surface was
captivating. We continued on to where the river
forked, there were no trees now and up this side
fork was Lady's Well, where people were
swimming. Cuddy was delighted to see me, he
was there with Doda, my other school friend
who had carrot red hair, freckles and tilted his
head to one side when he was talking. The little
fellow shook hands with them both, like big
people do. They laughed and winked at him and
asked him if he was going swimming. He said
no, he was not, as he has no togs with him and
he was going to play on the bank. We got into
our togs carefully and prudishly covering up
with towels, as there were women and girls
about too. The water was cold for a second but
then after a minute it was lovely and came up
just under the chin in the deepest part. There

was a big flat rock in the middle of the river just barely under the water that you could stand up and dive from and then swim under the water with your eyes open. Here I made a most important, most exciting discovery that women definitely didn't have mickeys. I saw that for myself as they swam ahead of me in their slips, the old ones had hair and the young ones had slits and I couldn't get enough of diving, double checking it all out. Then suddenly Cuddy was shouting at me from the bank that the little fellow had fallen in head first. I swam caught him and lifted him up to Cuddy, his eyes were huge and he was bawling for a little while. I got out and dried him with a towel. He didn't want his clothes taken off as people were all around. But Annie, a woman who worked helping my mother from time to time, was on the bank with some of her daughters and she gave me a dry vest and a knickers to put on the little fellow. He was disgusted at having to wear girls clothes. Cuddy and Doda came up to the road and while walking up with us I told them that girls didn't have mickeys and they all roared laughing at me including the little fellow. They were all saying, that they knew that ages ago. I felt a right fool and God punished me for looking by nearly drowning my little brother. I pedaled home fast as the little fellow was cold even with the towel wrapped around him, but we had a wonderful adventure.

The Affair

Is it chemistry or physics or both when that devilment purrs in the atmosphere creating an almost static electricity? Yes, that beautiful devilment that shook the tree in the garden so long ago, sparked by a knowing smile that got it trembling, a tongue tip wobbling on a pouting lip, a glint of come-hither in the eye. That scent, that wobbly scent that unhinges the normal rational behavioural response, is it some imagination or a reviving of an undeniable desire from the memory banks of some previous unfulfilled lifetime? Delightfully haunting, hurting, sore the images, tumbling, tauntingly that caught him, clutching his cell phone possessively as if she were within. God he wanted her now, her presence was singing inside him, awaiting embracement, possession, full occupancy, a drinking tasting union an unceasing restlessness.

He stopped to pause and remember her, her fair hair cut short, slightly bowl shaped and reminiscent of the urchin cut of the flower power days in the sixties. French chic, she was alluring in her well tailored outfit, exuding a refined sensuality. You knew she had the capacity to blossom into raw thumping lust when nurtured with care and imagination.

Naked nubile nuances, were the natural
nothings that expressed themselves in oils and
acrylics in forms exotic and erotic, in the private
sketch pad of her soul. She danced here bare-
chested wearing long black stockings and high
heels, to jazzy strains of a wailing saxophone
and a raunchy piano, provocatively beaming a
bold naughty kind of innocence.

Reggae beats from the Caribbean, bongo drums
from the tropic lands, laced with sitar rajas from
Rajasthan provided background for this woman
and –oh! I don't know!.

The left hand played low strong randy piano
while the right one stroked it slow and let you
know it could be so exciting. Yes arias from the
operas, passion pleasures, plaintiff strains
stretching strong the sayonaras from Othello
type love scenes, played out in night train
wanderings when she went out there in his
dreams.

Oh!,oh!, where was it going- in a few years her
kids would be left home and it wouldn't be so
painful - the charade was wearing she needed
love affection, attention, touch, appreciation, a
bit of sunshine, just to be able to wake up and
talk and hold someone that shares the same
longings that you can go travelling with and that
you needn't be on tippy-toe with, regarding
religion, or openness about the enjoyment of
sexual pleasure.

Was she in a happy marriage? It was ok! He was a good provider; he was into the parish community, the local GAA, the Local Gun Club, that took up most of his weekends. His mother was still calling a lot of shots in their lives, she wanted out without a fight but couldn't initiate the move and hadn't the nerve to even pretend to the kids or himself that the fun was gone. This affair was a fine state of affairs, she knew that he knew that she knew that he was interested and was just waiting for the word and he knew that she knew that he knew that it was likewise with her. They had held hands briefly, looked in one another's eyes, sighed, gasped, leaned into one another going out a doorway and finally exchanged cell phone numbers. No communication for two weeks until the night of the full moon and then it went back and forth for a couple of hours, until eventually they settled on what would be safe times for both of them, school days during the week and afternoons at the weekends. She got perky and he got horny and their lives began to change, she got horny and he got desperate and plans for some time together had to be made. Things came to a head out of the blue. At a Sunday lunch, a discussion at the table about the priests sermon on the abortion issue, the mother in law and her husband in full agreement with the holy celibate ignoramus. Furious she was as she pondered the fate of the poor child down the road, who was up the pole by a recently divorced big land owner.

He who had threatened to choke her in the four by four having picked her up hitching home from school. She was boiling and she blew, she let them both have it in front of the kids, the two eldest smiled their approval to her as she went upstairs. She threw a few clothes and a bit of make up into a bag. At the end of the stairs while throwing on her coat she told the kids that there was plenty of food in the fridge and she would be back when she cooled. Before she started the car in the driveway she texted - Lisdoonvarna This Evening.

The Gift

"Many a tear has to fall but it 's all in the game of love". The tinkling memory of that country western song playing loud and clear, the flashing coloured bulbs, the rumbling generators and machines, that twirled the chair planes and grumbled the dodgem cars on the metal floors while sparking the overhead electrified mesh, lit up a nomadic vista, with potential to travel in a circus of burlesque magic, for me the young impressionable. Pain and magic were on the agenda for growing up, and I was on the way. A horny excitement was growling within and this was happening before fagan stood proud to take over my teenage yearnings. Something was calling me –all this was private and not for adult endorsement or contemplation. Something wild and primitive got precedence invariably over all other ramblings in my internal dialogue. Instinct was rising to prominence and what society offered with its conformity was tame and unexciting. Hollywood movies were just propaganda glorifying the conformists. British movies spoke down with marble mouth and were not to be trusted. French movies were sometimes arty, thought provoking, and worthy of consideration, now and again. The war was over, they said. German, Japanese and Italian fascism had been vaguely exposed and defeated and the new villain was Communism – Socialism.

Confusion reigned in the adolescent mind. You had to believe in the God in the Frock with the Beard and the virgin so pure, so pure, so, so, pure, who was like your mother, who never, ever had sex. You yourself were another immaculate conception like Jesus. My parents never had sex, my little brother just arrived out of the blue. Lady Justice with the balance scales was lopsided in favour of rich rulers. A thirst was growing for some form of experiential conformation of truth, no one out there could be trusted. What about the Holy Ghost?! Did I believe in ghosts? Well, there was some energy running me other than my intellect. My grandmother was at ease from her yoga. Yoga was union. Union with what, yourself, your spirit? The search for spirit, to make me feel happy, content, satisfied, connected, real communion in other words. Well the journey was long, arduous and interesting. It had to come to the stage where you'd give all for the feeling of certainty. That pinnacle moment of clarity while indulging to the full in booze, hallucinating drugs, in religion, in sex, a pause. Alone with oneself to face the ensuing loneliness, emptiness and feelings of abandonment, all that was left besides suicidal thoughts, was resentment. Isolation ward private! That feeling meant, that once upon a time I had felt a connection to something. So the search was on again find the Guru to instruct in the yoga, the one to bring you from Gu to Ru, yes darkness to light. Authenticity with integrity was hard to ascertain but I knew from Kabir, Rumi, Tulsidas that Sat Guru was greater than God. Why? Because he revealed God within the individual. His duty was to manifest for the true devotee. So master is found, his presence is serene, tranquil, and full of love, incredible, but how do I get to hold on to it for myself. Now his gift to me was to show the source. That the light, the love, the peace, the joy, the happiness, was already there within me. He just revealed the techniques on how to get in. The greater the thirst the deeper it would be, but it required practice. He explained that he was just like a lit candle and that he had to remain lit in order to light others because he had taken on the job from the time of his father's death when he was eight years old. Lovely stories he told. When asked what gift he would ask for if he met a Genii, without hesitation he smiled that beautiful innocent smile "The greatest gift of all, the gift of devotion". Basically you had God by the short hairs if you had the gift of devotion, he had to come for the devotee.

Nerostrasse 1

Mon Dieu! Mon Dieu! What am I doing here,
talking to myself again. Here I am once again, in
Kranz Platz, infernal fiddle music burning and
scorching my shadow memory mind, the sound
of marching, " *Veni, Vidi, Vici*", "*Festina Lente*",
bemuddled I am in the steamy air. Coming out
of the spa somewhat light-headed on a whim on
an intuitive, instinctive kind of whim I head
straight for revisiting Nerostrasse. The Jazz
House on my left looks familiar, as does the
Quellenhoff Inn with the same old doormat that
always tripped me up. Strange after so long. I
am walking up the street and look back through
the Jazz house door which is wide open and I'd
swear that was Mick and Red in the leather
pilot's jacket with the fur collar - weird. It's near
fifty years ago when the German mark was
worth about one and ten pence or *cent trente* in
French money. Strange – even the old Taunus
looks familiar. I continue towards No.39 on the
right and there it is, the brass knocker, letterbox
and doorbell still shiny and smelling of polish. I
ring, hearing a familiar old sound as I note the
well worn limestone doorstep. I hear rapid
footsteps and then the door is opened by a
woman in her late thirties, her hair up in a hair
net with an old-fashioned wrap around apron
overall.

There is a shimmering about her countenance, her lipstick is odd and there are smudges of rouge on her cheeks. She shakily angles the head to eye me *"Nach mall Herr Connell hast kine schlussel huh! Kompt.*

I am ushered in, I know the voice, it's Frau Bender, the old landlady, but she is younger now than she was then. I am confused and put my hand on the banister to steady myself but my hand passed right through it as I stumble and correct myself. The silence is full of sound like high volume static. The refracted light through the stain glass window over the front door is dancing dappled light, intensely giving a kaleidoscopic appearance and motion to everything in the hallway. An air of uncertainty and unreality has engulfed me and instinctively I grope towards the familiar, which was the door to my right. This led to a courtyard, and the enjoining building where I presumed Frau Bender had disappeared, towards the stairway and up four flights to my old attic loft room. My footsteps echoed loudly under the archway in the cobbled courtyard, reviving a memory, an embarrassing memory, of staggering up the four flights of stairs with my stoppered six litre bottles of beer in a brown paper bag.
While fumbling for my key on the upper stairway I had stumbled, the bag slipped and plunged the four flights to the awaiting echo chamber of a courtyard exploding and awakening my neighbours.

Admonished I was and warned of the evils of too much drink! Here I was again with the memory still chastening me as I climbed skywards. Panting and out of breath I reach my old room and clutch the half palm sized schlussel to turn and open the door. As before the room is half taken up by the big bed and eider quilt. There is a pot bellied stove, a chest of drawers, a tall press, a chair, a wooden box for a table, and a green mossy skylight, veined purple and crimson where a second sheet of glass was superimposed on the cracked one, as a patch job. The prevailing odour was that of mothballs and coal dust. I closed my eyes and sat down on the bed. Memories kept swirling dizzyingly, emotionally charged with unrequited love, male challenges, loud laughter, female tear shedding, raucous revelry, occupational anxiety and home sickness to a background of Offenbach and beirkeller music, in carnival colours. I lay down on the pillow, kicking off my shoes as I stretched into a deep sleep or something.. …

The coarse material has caused a chaffing on my elbows, I am leaning over a manuscript busy, intent, focused, writing and illustrating a prophetic scene - a rocky grove of shrubby trees by a stream with rippling water gently frushing over pebbles. A large benign looking serpent is curled on a tree stump by a basket of rosy apples.

A sensuous woman in a golden gossamer chiffon like garment outlining her breasts, nipples, and pubic rotundity, is idly stroking an attentive wolfhound, while her eyes have a far away look of some loneliness. The words on the manuscript are in Gaelic "*Má bhíon scammal sa speir,bhí chinte go bhfuil uigneas san anam*" if there is a cloud in the sky be sure that there is loneliness in the soul. I am now above my body looking down on myself, dressed in an oatmeal habit, a plaited rope around my waist, and open toed leather sandals on my feet. My face is weatherworn, and bearded, my skull is tonsured, very dark with a hint of grey and I am humming contentedly at my work. A dragon fly has landed on the open page and I accept him as a portrait offering for the leaf I am illustrating. It's busy I get with my coloured inks, precious dyes, the blue lapis lazuli for the dragon fly has come overland from Badakhshan in Afghanistan, to capture the presented detail. The female devours the male after copulation. I pause, reflect, conject, and smile ruefully as I scan inwardly. Insect, bird, animal, human - nature devouring all assumptions of power. I suck my testicles towards my groin in silent confirmation and gentle affirmation of my temporary adherence to celibacy. There is less to worry about when one has greater freedom for speculation, as the coiled snake most benign in his demeanour, yet most powerful in his muscular propensity. Behind his head four prominent black definitive diamonds shine forth most forcibly denoting the shape shifting capacity of this Joker! Harlequin! dimension changer, the one that lurks behind the squeezing and skin shedding capacity, to metamorphose practically on whim. Power beings, like a cat with nine lives and its tail constantly twitched, eyes keenly alert. The wolfhound enjoying the woman's attention retains his alertness to the serpent's proximity as portrayed by the bristling hairs round his neck. As too, one of the apples at the edge of the basket shows that someone has taken a hefty bite and left the apple back. Alert and aware I am of merging and emerging of presence with attachment and presence with detachment simultaneous connection and instantaneous reaction to and from separate life forces animate and seemingly inanimate. The pen has been busy in it's detail, portraying, shading and outlining a multiplicity of mood interpretations and all are yet instantaneously subject to change as one notices the tip of the woman's tongue teasingly protruding, just that tiny little bit. Loneliness, so near so far as I exhale, while on inhalation contentment reigns as I ruminate and scratch and itch with utter satisfaction. ."Life is like an asses gallop - short and sweet" me thinks, each moment full of unique potential, the capacity to choose change and alter direction at will. Such a freedom aught not be ignored. A bell is pealing, beckoning contentment, offering food and gratifying company in chanting and unification in meditation.

Nerostrasse 2

Chapter 2. *Om Namo Shiva I a. Om Om buíochas le Dia* – Golden light internally shimmering - that special feeling of an awesome trembling gratitude for awareness of an added dimension to my human existence. Feeling happy and content like a labrador dog having just emerged from the river with a jerking salmon firmly clutched in his teeth, pausing to shake off the surplus water, wagging his tail ecstatically in his excitement and pride of pinnacle achievement. Am I a dog or a monk? *Shur*, one is as good as the other when one knows one is alive and one is being gifted breath after breath, in contented connection to nature. The sound of the bell is still resonating in the remembrance, vibrating membranes in the skeleton that connects to elements in old star dust, time and travel merely maya. The old sandals shuffle towards the scent of steaming vegetables and baked spelt bread from the beaconing refectory. Entering in unison with some older monks, I incline my head in a silent deference to age and experience as we go to wash hands and feet before eating. In these silent moments just before Grace, where everyone is seated with eyes closed in quiet contemplation and thanksgiving, my stomach rumbles loudly proclaiming my covert animal voraciousness. I blush with some embarrassment while my brother monks smile indulgently, probably noting the remnants of pride that lurk behind my humble façade.

This mind of mine needs cleansing if I am ever to be at peace. I bite a chunk of bread and slowly masticate, my mind mulls with "*mens sana in corporae sano*" a healthy mind in a healthy body. Circulation and elimination, liver and kidneys, the primary organs in that regard. And what about spirit, the Holy Ghost " (*an Spioraid Naofa*) or maybe a drop of the *creathur* to ease the strain ..Why endure? Pain is inevitable, but suffering is optional. A state of mind like paradise I suppose – "A place or state where the blessed see and enjoy?!" Rumbling and grumbling internally I spoon the warm vegetables and soak the broth with the crusts contentedly savouring while silently sighing, a mourning keening for the retreating hunger. Strange that! Hunger keeps one sharp and far more alert to priorities. Give priorities to what – what is? – Hm? I am that I am, a bit of sustenance around breath. Surrender that mind that blade of intellect, surrender and feel. My eyes close to a warm embrace of a soft and gentle internal light and a tinkling sound like crickets at twilight, all comfortably murmuring acknowledgement and devotion to life. To life so deeply nourishing and satisfying that I grunt my gratitude breaking the evening silence. Some of the older monks smirk their bemusement, while the younger ones remain hang -jawed for a while. I stand, stretch and breathe in rhythm and unison with the vespers that have already commenced in my own internal dialogue - the animal inclining towards the divine intention. Entering the scented chamber, absorbing the tranquil presence, my body relaxes as my nostrils flare and some form of *pranyama* automatically settles me in readiness for chanting healing mantras. Yes, yoga it is, union without a doubt, union being at one, no feeling of being separated or isolated. * *Aontacht*, a special feeling of uniqueness felt by the heart, with the head bowed and intellect in submission to awesome feelings of gratitude. A lovely space to enter, dwell and partake in connection. I take my seat in the bench and await commencement as the remainder of the monks take their places. The first note takes me right out and I let it. Hovering, *ag folaim san aer*, visible, invisible amidst the cloud wisps, just pulsating energy with vision, gifted to view to partake and behold the scene, about, above, below, without and within. An unrestricted spirit smiles benevolently without arrogance or uniqueness, fluttering in acquiescence and aware acceptance, knowing the awareness was gifted and not earned. While soaring and shimmering the intellect invades the spirit, to addle and question it in it's demand for centre stage. With whom and where is this gifter? How and to whom do I address my gratitude? Some birds fly by in celestial harmony singing the praises in answering enlightenment. As each breath deepens, and lengthens by multiples, my shoulder blades start to ache and I slowly realize my arms are fully outstretched and are moving rhythmically. It is physically cold, my eyes are closed, and yet I am seeing, while my nerve ends seem to have shot out quite some distance from my extremities, proclaiming my ability to aviate effortlessly with primordial memory at the helm.

133

For a brief moment my mind attempts to analyze and rationalize the incomprehensible time warp and transmogrification but my survival instinct shut out the unnecessary as I glided unerringly on the up currents. Spirit we surely are, much more so than a confined being embodied and limited to a time zone.

Again the bell rings a resonance to alter atomic confirmation with energetic metamorphose, sound to light, to matter, and antimatter and antiparticle like a call to fast forward towards some form of virtuous deorivation with telepathic entitlements.

*pranyama: yogic breathing
* Aontacht: being at one with

To Be Contd........"dan de dan dan da- there is a horse between my thighs, my left hand is outstretched before me holding an imaginary reins I am beating my own ass to the rhythm of my pounding heels as I escape out of Mc Graths Cinema after the Sunday afternoon matinee in Thurles town - It's 1946 and the war is over." Will I ever grow up?

Trainboy

While rumbling on the Varanasi Express from Lokmanya, Mumbai to Kashi, Banaras, Varanasi (all names for the oldest inhabited city on this planet), the cultural capital of India, and home to Kabir and Ravidas, where Gautama Buddha gave his first sermon, yes, I have always had some remarkably enlightening experience en route and this time it was no different. Traveling in old carriages that clanked and rattled, that shifted, shunted and shuddered noisily, rhythmically, with smells and odors of spice, dung, urine, perfume, incense, curry and masala chai, amidst lovely curious soft, gentle and respectful people, I rocked harmoniously within, childishly getting more excited as I neared my favorite city. A globe of blue light intensifies behind my dozing eyelid, prompted me to take notice. A large head sat on a frail looking angular body with matchstick legs poking awkwardly out of dirty badly stained khaki trousers. His lip hung low on the left side showing a slight drool. Huge quizzical brown eyes scrutinized attentively, yet aggressively, in a squinting and flaring fashion. A short sleeved small boys check cotton shirt with open neck he wore, the colors were bright, it looked freshly washed. Something resembling a zinc miraculous medal on a dirty blue thread or twine hung under his chin.

He moved deftly and quickly towards the corner by the window seat, he pulled a little hand broom of bound twigs from under his oxter and diligently swept crumbs, fruit peels, clay, papers, and red dust neatly towards the corridor alternately bouncing on his hands and tucking the brush under his oxter. I was stunned with his speed and dexterity as I realized his feet were folded lotus like for convenience and not for conveyance. Sad knowledge tells me he was probably custom crippled for begging purposes. Our eyes had met maybe four times as he swept through the small compartment and under my seat, they were furtive darting, inquisitive, cautious, defensive looks. He checked that no one was looking and while bouncing towards the corridor exit he flexed quickly his thumb, forefinger, and middle finger before his lips signifying a near constant state of famishment. My emotions were quivering to buy him off with a coin, a note, this teenage boy equal in age to my own boy equal in tragedy to my parents and grandparents collectively. I rose and groped my wallet and moved to the corridor with him. He became extremely fretful in the corridor and I realized the train conductor might also be a poncing parasite, a preying vulture on the vulnerable. I rolled a note carefully tightly round a biro refill and reinserted it. He watched this cheap broken biro being dropped for his little broom.

The dazzling flash of approval, gratitude, admiration, directed towards me was indescribable; it was delivered in the flicker of a moment and immediately returned to the mask and the serious business at hand. In a moment bounced into the next compartment.

Thank Yous

Sincere thanks to the writer's groups in Kinvara, Ennis, Castlebar, and Westport. Thanks to John Colohan for his patience time and expertise while recording. Thank you Tony O'Connell who was so patient regarding publishing essentials *agus buíochas do Eugene chuig an cabhair a glach sé gan stint* and last but not least is Ritaji whose gentle love, truth, kindness, and saintly acceptance continues to rescue the demon who persists in willful resurrection.

Thank you the reader, we were one, once in the time warp of existence, and I hope my gratitude in truth extends to enhance and to continue traveling in body and spirit form.

www.donaloconnell.com

Donal O'Connell lives on an organic holding in Turlough, Bellharbour, in the heart of the Burren, a unique area in County Clare, Ireland.

Made in the USA
Charleston, SC
23 August 2013